# *Human Resources Outsourcing*

## Solutions, suppliers, key processes and the current market

## *A case-study-based market review*

*Ian Hunter*
*Jane Saunders*

Published by
Gower Publishing Limited
Gower House
Croft Road
Aldershot
Hampshire
GU11 3HR
England

Gower Publishing Company
Suite 420
101 Cherry Street
Burlington
VT 05401-4405
USA

Ian Hunter and Jane Saunders have asserted their moral right under the Copyright, Designs and Patents Act, 1988, to be identified as the authors of this work.

British Library Cataloguing in Publication Data
    Hunter, Ian, 1963-
        Human resources outsourcing : solutions, suppliers, key
        processes and the current market
        1. Personnel management - Contracting out - Europe
        I. Title II. Saunders, Jane
        658.3'0094

    ISBN-13: 9780566088018

Library of Congress Control Number:  2007928568

Printed and bound in Great Britain by TJ International Ltd, Padstow, Cornwall.

# Contents

# ACKNOWLEDGEMENTS

Orion Partners would like to acknowledge and thank the assistance given by Angela Cha of Pinsent Masons for her help in developing the section of this report which deals with legal structures. Angela specializes in business process outsourcing, HR & IT outsourcings and major IT projects.

We would also like to record our thanks to Mircea Albeanu, Colina Greenway, Martin Hunt, Nicola Swan and Catherine Purcell, all of Orion Partners, who helped in the preparation and production of this report.


Ian Hunter and Jane Saunders

# 1. EXECUTIVE SUMMARY

This report was prepared by Orion Partners and provides an overview of the market for HR outsourcing services in Europe since the late 1990s. The report also addresses the main considerations for an organisation considering a large-scale transference of HR transactional activity to an outsource provider of HR outsourcing (HRO).

## *THE MARKET*

Orion Partners estimate that the global size of the full service HRO market covers more than 128 deals with a combined value in excess of US$23 billion. The global leaders are Hewitt with 33 deals worth US$7.8 billion, Accenture with 21 deals worth US$4.9 billion and ACS with 8 deals worth US$2.5 billion. The majority of these deals have a North American focus.

The European market for full-scope HR transactional outsourcing, covering all parts of the employee life-cycle, is still relatively immature compared to North America but is showing signs of acceleration, particularly in mainland Europe.

> **European Market – Key Facts**
>
> - European market relatively immature – 70% HRO deals are first generation deals for over 25 000 employees
>
> - UK represents 50% of the European market which has grown threefold over the past 5 years
>
> - Public sector accounts for 19% of the European market
>
> - Deals have typically taken 18 months to 3 years but are speeding up
>
> - Average contract terms are 8 years with breakpoints at 3–5 years
>
> - Average European contract value US$300m

At present, the market is still focused mainly on first generation deals to organisations of over 25 000 employees; this market accounts for 70% of European deals. The public sector market is steadily growing with 19% of European deals coming from this sector, as well as an increasing number of single service line deals in the UK, which may lead to full HRO if proven successful.

Historically, the complexity of HRO deals has led to long negotiation and transition timescales (18 months to 3 years were not untypical) but signs are that outsourcers are becoming more efficient at the process of transition and this timescale is rapidly coming down.

Overall the HRO market is maturing quickly with a significant increase in signed deals in 2005 and 2006 versus the previous period 1998–2004. Some high-profile first generation deals (for example, BP and BT) have been renewed once the initial deal term expired (although in BP's case not with the same supplier). There is abundance evidence that HRO deals have delivered on their promised cost savings (typically a reduction of at least 20%) but have not realized the ambitions of transforming the strategic value of HR's service delivery or enabled the retained HR function to increase its profile and perceived value as a business partner.

HRO suppliers are split between those with specific expertise in the HR domain and those who provide HRO as part of a broader spectrum of outsourced/managed services. Although there has been some consolidation of key players, the supplier market appears relatively stable at present. Eleven of the main HRO providers are profiled in this report.

**Trends**

- Significant growth evidenced during 2005 and 2006

- Capita/BBC deal announced in February 2006 and Accenture/Unilever in June 2006

- 17% increase in worldwide HRO predicted for 2007

- Average price per employee - US$325 (down 55% since 1998)

- Predicted increase in 'multi-tower', cross-functional deals.

**Main providers**

- Top five providers in terms of global capability, offshore resources, size and breadth of portfolio are:
  - Accenture
  - ACS
  - Fidelity
  - Hewitt
  - IBM

- Hewitt are global leaders in HR BPO

- Accenture lead market in Europe

- Speculation about a merger between Accenture/Hewitts

## SCOPE OF SERVICES

Evidence suggests that there is no 'ideal' scope of outsourced services; this is typically subject to negotiation. However, an examination of existing deals reveals where the distinctions are generally made between frequently outsourced, occasionally outsourced and rarely outsourced services.

This analysis suggests that HRO rarely impacts elements of the HR service such as:

- HR policy and strategy development;
- HR business partnering;
- recruitment authority and selection decisions;
- employee relations/collective bargaining;
- strategic training needs and talent management;
- exit/severance decisions.

## THE IMPLICATIONS OF HRO FOR RETAINED HR

Evidence suggests that outsourcing organisations frequently underestimate the impact of HRO on the retained HR function. A lack of clarity around retained HR roles leads to uncertainty and a tendency to act as a 'double-check' on the outsourcer instead of focusing on strategic, value-enhancing services.

Depending on the extent to which 'specialist and advisory' services are included in the outsource arrangements, the ratio of support for the retained HR function can fall from less than one retained HR full-time equivalent per 250 employees (1:250) to more than 1:1000+.

Key considerations for the retained function in the HRO process include:

- Integration of service delivery, business objectives and strategy (*the service led design concept*);
- developing a clear view of unique or business specific activities that cannot be effectively outsourced;
- differentiation of discrete, self-sufficient processes from embedded processes that are complex/costly to extract from the business;
- the extent to which routine HR management is delegated into the 'line'.

In managing the transition to the new service it is important for the retained service to establish the scope and rate of change most appropriate to the organisation. Different elements of the HRO service can and should be developed at a pace appropriate to the delivery of benefits and the management of risk.

The retained function will need to take on new tasks, principally the management of the external service provider and their performance. This is likely to demand new roles in the function, such as 'Account Manager' and 'Service Analyst', to manage service governance. Relationship management must, typically, be a jointly owned process that focuses on:

- Developing the service in line with changes to business strategy;
- flexing the service to meet operational demand;
- measurement and reporting on service performance;
- providing formal service management forums.

The move to HRO will considerably change the traditional career paths for HR and historic routes to senior positions via transactional services have to be reconsidered. Secondments and transfers to/from the outsource providers may offer the potential for a full breadth of professional development opportunities. In addition HRO typically stimulates demand for new career paths and new skill sets in the organisation – for example:

- Contract management;
- business planning;
- internal consultancy;
- career management.

## CONTRACTUAL OPTIONS FOR DELIVERY OF HRO

Multiple options have emerged for structuring contracts with an HRO provider. The key considerations will include:

- Client concerns/demands for simplicity in the deal;
- approaches to risk management;
- cost of service;
- requirements for 'best in class' services versus the 'one stop shop' approach;
- the potential to realise VAT savings through the structure of the deal.

Six variations of HRO contract are considered here including:

- Simple 'classic' arrangements with a single service provider;
- a single service provider utilising multiple sub-contracted services;
- multi-sourcing arrangements with several service providers;
- multiple service providers operating through a single joint venture operation (a special purpose vehicle (SPV) consortium);
- customer/service provider SPV joint venture delivering some tax advantages;
- sourcing services via a company-owned shared services subsidiary.


## THE TRANSITION PROCESS

Experience suggests that the transition to the new service is one of the most demanding aspects of the outsourcing process. The approach taken to this aspect of the outsource deal will determine the success of the arrangement as well as the tone of future dealings with the supplier.

Typically transition activities take from 9 months to more than 24 months to conclude. The trend is for transition to be completed within 12 months in order to drive out early benefits and to avoid the disruption to business that a long transition may incur.

The transition to the new service must achieve four main objectives:

- Agreeing the contract for services;
- transferring operational responsibility to the service provider;
- transferring staff to the service provider;
- establishing the technical infrastructure.

The transition process involves the integration and management of multiple work streams including:

- Programme management;
- change management, people and communications;
- financial management;
- service management;
- transfer of operations;
- technology delivery.

Multiple factors can affect the timing and tasks involved in the transition process, specific examples include:

- Decisions about whether to effect transformation activity before or after the transition;
- whether the outsourcing process will need to develop new greenfield services or will focus on transfer of existing services;
- approaches to funding the HRO deal;
- the scope of services outsourced and the relative risk of failure in each area.

There are multiple potential risks to the transition process. However, common problems that may be avoided and should be addressed early in the process include:

- Limited contract negotiation skills and experience in the internal team;
- lack of resources and skills available in-house to support the change management programme;
- poor communication and lack of continuity with existing third party HR suppliers during transition;
- the potential loss of key staff during transition;
- underestimation of the effort required by the internal team/stakeholders and the knock-on impact on 'business as usual' activities as well as the ability of the organisation to absorb the total amount of change taking place; so called 'change bandwidth capacity'.

Successful transition demands a clear split of responsibilities between the service provider and the client. Outsourcing organisations are likely to require specialist support during transition but must also develop internal capability to manage their risk.

**Top Ten Tips for HR Outsourcing**

*Before an organisation embarks on outsourcing its HR function it should have:*

1. identified how outsourcing fits with strategic objectives;

2. agreed which core strategic competencies must be kept in-house and what can safely be outsourced;

3. identified a complete view of internal HR service delivery costs; the main cost drivers and the potential savings and investment;

4. assessed 'internal outsourcing' and explored how shared services might deliver the same benefits but with greater retained control;

5. identified the technological challenges and solutions around outsourcing – for example, have the full costs of running and retiring legacy systems been calculated accurately?

6. developed a clear view about the capabilities and reputation of each of the main outsourcing providers;

7. standardized and simplified processes and procedures prior to considering outsourcing;

8. discussed in detail the concept of outsourcing with customers (employees and business managers) and other key stakeholders in the organisation;

9. defined the key success measures that will be used to judge the performance of the outsource provider and the structure of the deal;

10. considered the history of the organisation in terms of managing complex transition processes – is there the organisational will to see an outsourcing initiative through to completion?

# 2. INTRODUCTION

This report provides an overview of the main developments in the growth of the market for HR outsourcing in Europe since the late 1990s. HR outsourcing is not a new phenomenon. Individual HR services such as recruitment, payroll and training delivery have a long and proven record of successful provision via specialist third party providers. What the emergence of organisations such as Exult and Xchanging established was a new market for full-scope HRO transactional outsourcing which covered all parts of the employee life cycle administration as well as deep line manager and employee advisory services. This report focuses on the full-scope HRO deals and providers rather than the plethora of single service line outsourcing suppliers.

The report is structured as follows:

- Overview of the European HRO market covering the major deals signed since 1998, the principle providers and specific details about the major public sector contracts that have been signed to date.
- Summary of what HR services are frequently, occasionally and rarely outsourced based on the deals that have been signed to-date.
- Review of the implications for the retained HR function which highlights the options for focusing the efforts of the professional HR community who remain out of scope of the HRO deal.
- Summary of the main contractual options that have been used to structure outsourcing deals (from the straightforward supplier/customer arrangement to the more complex special purpose vehicle/joint venture options).
- Review of the common approaches to managing the transition of services and people to the new arrangements including indicative timings, risks and issues.
- The appendices provide detailed vendor information and a deal summary of the major and minor HRO deals over the last 8 years and more detailed case studies of the deals between:

  o BT/Accenture
  o BP/Hewitt (Exult)
  o AFPAA (Armed Forces)/ExcellerateHRO (EDS/Towers Perrin)
  o Westminster City Council/Vertex (United Utilities)
  o Unilever/Accenture
  o Lloyds TSB/Xansa

# 3. OVERVIEW OF THE EUROPEAN MARKET SIZE AND GROWTH

Orion Partners estimate that the global size of the full service HR outsourcing (HRO) market covers more than 128 deals with a combined value in excess of US$23 billion. The global leaders are Hewitt with 31 deals worth US$7.8 billion, Accenture with 21 deals worth US$4.9 billion and ACS with 8 deals worth US$2.5 billion. The majority of these deals have a North American focus and the market for full service HRO in Europe is relatively immature.

This immaturity is reflected in the fact that, of the European HRO deals signed to date, almost 70% of European HRO transactions are first-generation 'mega-deals' with organisations employing over 25 000 people.

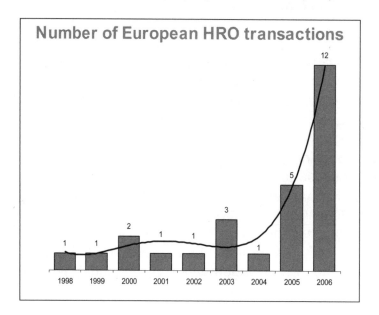

*Source: Orion Partners*

Whilst the earliest European HRO transactions were all in the UK, in the last few years there has been significant activity in continental Europe, with approximately 90% of transactions in mainland Europe. However, the UK still represents almost 50% of the market by transaction value, which reflects the broader scope and complexity of UK deals. There has also been an increase in the number of global deals signed in North America that have a European footprint.

To date most European deals have been made in high-tech and telecommunications, manufacturing, financial and government sectors. Public sector transactions have risen from 7% to 19% with a steady growth in the number of smaller 'single service line' deals in this sector which may well lead to full HPO if successfully implemented.

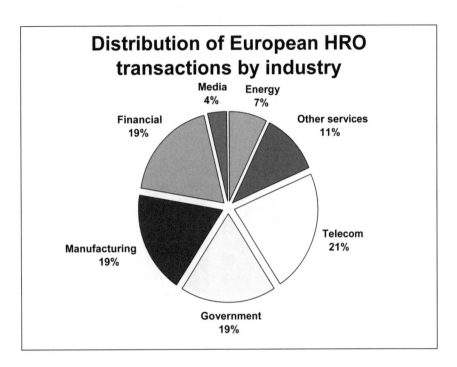

**Distribution of European HRO transactions by industry**

Media 4%
Energy 7%
Financial 19%
Other services 11%
Telecom 21%
Manufacturing 19%
Government 19%

**Source: Orion Partners**

Steady total contract value (TCV) growth evidenced since the late 1990s is now showing a sharp increase as a consequence of major deals during 2006 resulting from the US$1 billion Accenture/Unilever, US$250 million Capita/BBC and US$500 million Accenture/BT implementations as well as major public sector deals, particularly the US$346 million Fujitsu/Northern Ireland Dept. of Finance and Personnel and US$380 million Agilsys/Rochdale Metropolitan Borough Council contracts.

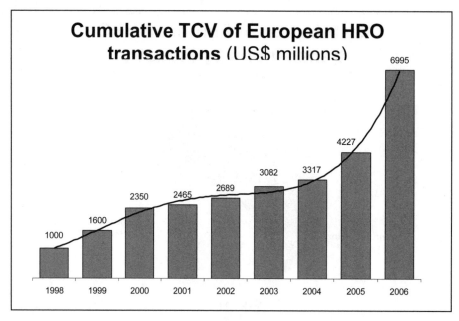

Note: Sample 23 contracts (6 estimated values)

*Source: Orion Partners*

The trend for large 'mega-deals' shows no evidence of slowing down with the average 'employees supported' in 2006 running at almost 50 000 per contract. Whilst the Unilever deal with 200 000 employees is unusual, IKEA and Lloyds TSB account for a further 150 000.

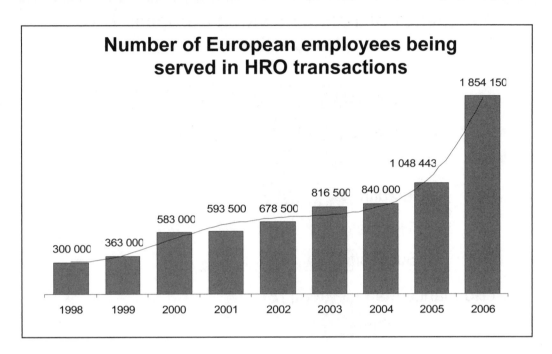

**Number of European employees being served in HRO transactions**

| Year | Number |
|------|--------|
| 1998 | 300 000 |
| 1999 | 363 000 |
| 2000 | 583 000 |
| 2001 | 593 500 |
| 2002 | 678 500 |
| 2003 | 816 500 |
| 2004 | 840 000 |
| 2005 | 1 048 443 |
| 2006 | 1 854 150 |

*Source: Orion Partners*

Possible reasons for slow growth during the early years include the total or partial unwinding of some of the initial deals and long lead times (typically 18 months to 3 years) to contract as both suppliers and buyers get to grips with the complexities that must be overcome to achieve a successful HRO. Both of these are reflective of the newness of the market but more recent deals indicate that early teething problems are being resolved, resulting in an upswing in activity and an increase in the speed of progress in closing deals.

The average contract value for European deals is US$300 million and the average contract term is just under 8 years. The significant up front investment required to achieve both transformation in services and cost savings mean that pay back periods for suppliers are long.

Payback data, given its understandable confidential nature, is difficult to obtain, however, a major 2006 European 5-year deal was expecting payback within 4 years and DuPont anticipate productivity gains of 30% after 5 years following their deal with Convergys. Typically, contracts will have a breakpoint between year 3 and year 5 of the deal which will allow for a price review, the customer to break the deal and then either revert to in-house services or offer the contract to another supplier.

Although the range of HR services in scope varies significantly (see section 5), the majority of European HRO arrangements cover payroll, workforce administration and HR systems.

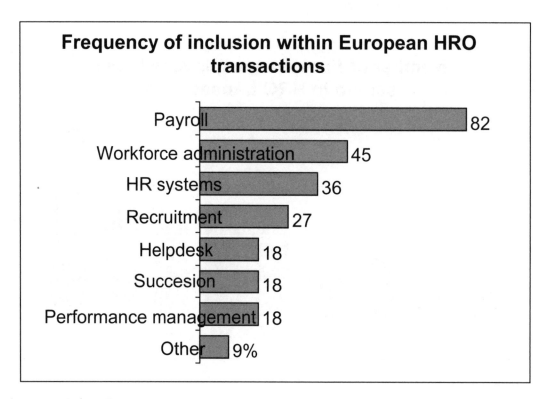

**Frequency of inclusion within European HRO transactions**

- Payroll: 82
- Workforce administration: 45
- HR systems: 36
- Recruitment: 27
- Helpdesk: 18
- Succesion: 18
- Performance management: 18
- Other: 9%

*Source: Orion Partners*

# KEY PROVIDERS

HRO suppliers fall broadly into two categories: those with core expertise in the HR domain and those diversifying from an IT/general business process outsourcing heritage. The industry has gone through a period of consolidation as players bid for market leadership. Although further consolidation is expected, the supplier market is currently relatively stable.

Appendix A contains a comprehensive listing of significant European HRO deals in the last 8 years.

## LEADING PROVIDERS

### ACCENTURE

At present, Accenture is the European market leader in multi-service HRO. Accenture is a truly global provider of IT and outsourcing solutions for a broad range of business functions, including HR. Accenture HR Services offers 'best total cost human resource solutions' using its consulting strength to develop transformational HR messages and its technology and service know-how to deliver cost savings. Accenture actively seeks to leverage its broad outsourcing expertise by bundling a number of business process outsourcing (BPO) offerings.

Accenture's Government Consulting Group is active in the UK market, with government contracts accounting for 10–15% of Accenture's business in 2004. The majority of these contracts have been in the IT arena and some have attracted controversy due to delays and cost overruns. To date Accenture has not won a UK public sector HRO but it has experience in other territories, for example its 2002 deal to provide comprehensive HRO for the US Transportation Security Administration.

In Europe, Accenture has signed major HRO deals with Telecom Italia, Cable & Wireless and BT, among others. The BT deal, signed in 2001 with a contract value of US$500 million, saw a joint venture between BT and Accenture, 'e-peopleserve'. Accenture bought BT out the following year and the re-branded e-peopleserve forms the backbone of what is now Accenture HR Services. Accenture's contract with BT was renewed early in 2005.

In December 2005, Accenture closed a US$150 million HR and procurement BPO deal with the Bank of Ireland and in June 2006 announced a groundbreaking US$1 billion deal with Unilever for IT, HR, finance and administration services making it the world's largest BP HRO contract on an annual billing basis.

## HEWITT (FORMERLY EXULT)

Hewitt is the recognized global market leader in large HR BPO but as yet has failed to achieve the same dominance in the European market. Hewitt's strength lies in its strong HR domain expertise, with a comprehensive HR consulting practice. It has leveraged its experience as a benefits administrator to develop an outsourcing business and in 2004 it acquired HR BPO pioneer Exult. HR BPO generated 65% of a total US$2.2 billion turnover in fiscal year 2004.

Although there are no reported full service BPO deals for Hewitt in the public sector in Europe, it offers extensive consulting services to the public sector in the US with its Federal Consulting practice and has developed a range of tailored payroll products to deal with UK public sector pay structures. The Hewitt UK HRO sales team are reportedly reluctant to pursue public sector contracts due to the perceived complexity and lengthy timelines of the procurement process that is sometimes seen in the public sector.

Globally Hewitt's HRO client list includes Prudential Financial Corp, Unisys, Sony and Air Canada. In the UK, Exult signed a landmark deal with BP for the first global end-to-end HR deal. (See further commentary in Appendix B).

## ACS

ACS has built a diversified BPO business from a core expertise in IT outsourcing. Traditionally a large scale, low cost transactional outsourcer, it is now seeking to move up the value chain and extend its footprint beyond North America. In mid 2005 it acquired MellonHR, strengthening its proposition as an end-to-end HRO provider, but it remains to be seen whether it can leverage Mellon's domain expertise to deliver more transformational solutions.

ACS has strong public sector BPO experience in the US, where deals include administration of child support payments and electronic road toll passes as well as recruitment, training and employer services.

In Europe, ACS signed an HRO contract for payroll, benefits and HR administration with GM Europe in 2003 worth US$210 million in 2003. In 2002 it entered into a contract with Motorola for a US$650 million 10-year global contract which includes services to European employees.

## IBM

Already the market leader in IT outsourcing, IBM entered the HRO arena by purchasing PwC's outsourcing business in 2002. IBM's brand and sheer size, with revenues of almost US$100 billion and 330 000 employees, means it is an almost automatic shortlist choice for any significant HRO deal.

IBM has extensive UK public sector experience, with a 10-year contract with Surrey County Council for administrative and customer facing services. It also has infrastructure contracts with Bradford, Hampshire, Oxfordshire and Flintshire and significant involvement in the e-Government programme.

Perhaps IBM's most notable HRO deal is the 10 year US$400 million contract agreed in 2003 with Proctor & Gamble to support almost 98 000 employees in nearly 80 countries, including 12 in Europe. IBM have been very active in Europe during 2006 and are rumoured to have a number of major new contracts to announce in early 2007.

## FIDELITY

Fidelity Employee Services Company (FESCo) is a relative newcomer to the HR BPO market, signing a contract with IBM as recently as 2002 forming a strategic alliance with the IT services giant. This was followed by a further deal, enabling Fidelity to acquire use of IBM's HR and Payroll application, HR Access, allowing them to target the growing European market with a product developed in Europe itself.

Fidelity has continued to develop HR Access making it the backbone of its BPO delivery platform.

Major clients include ABB, Bank of America, BASF and IBM; these four businesses alone accounting for some 650,000 employees/retirees with a massive 11 000 000 across its entire client base. However, it must be recognized that these numbers are swollen by the inclusion of retirement and pension planning schemes. A more realistic comparison is Fidelity's estimated 12% global market share of employees supported by full HR BPO arrangements.

Fidelity's competitive strength is largely as a result of its determination to deliver services off a standardized platform with all the associated economies of scale not least of which is 'price competitiveness'. Needless to say, for some clients this may well be a disincentive if they are looking for maximum flexibility.

A further considerable strength is their ability to access markets off the back of an acknowledged financial services strength which provides a sound basis for moving across industry boundaries, which when considered alongside a standard platform makes Fidelity a considerable force.

## *OTHER MAJOR PROVIDERS*

### ADP

ADP offers a range of BPO solutions, including services targeting the brokerage, automotive dealership and insurance claims markets. Its Employer

Services business runs the payroll for one in six private sector employees in the United States and ADP has built on this expertise to offer full-service HRO with its comprehensive outsourcing service.

ADP has partnered with SAP on its GlobalView payroll and HR administration service for large domestic and multinational companies, now being used by 32 multinationals in over 20 countries, and in July 2006 announced a major deal with IKEA covering administration and payroll for an undisclosed TCV.

## EDS/ExcellerateHRO

ExcellerateHRO was established in 2005 as a joint venture between EDS and Towers Perrin. ExcellerateHRO consists of Towers Perrin's pensions and benefits administration services together with EDS's payroll and HR outsourcing business. ExcellerateHRO has contracts (from single service to full HRO) with over 400 companies worldwide, serving 33 million active and retired workers.

EDS has a global reach and technological expertise which has made it a leading global provider of BPO services. The addition of Towers Perrin's HR domain expertise should make it a strong challenger to Hewitt's global market leadership going forward.

Like Accenture, EDS has a number of high profile IT outsourcing contracts with the UK government, and also like Accenture, some of these deals have run into difficulty (contracts with the Child Support Agency and Department of Work and Pensions have hit the headlines), ExcellerateHRO has secured an HRO contract with the Armed Forces Personnel Administration Agency, valued at £600 million over 10 years. (See Appendix B for further detail).

## ARINSO

ARINSO is a Belgian-based HR services provider with a strong European footprint. In January this year it acquired OpenHR, a provider of pre-packaged eHR templates and solutions.

Reported European deals for ARINSO include a 5-year contract with ACS signed in 2003, payroll outsourcing in 2005 for the 1 200 employees of Dutch pension fund PGGM, payroll services for Sodexho Germany and a 6-year deal with Bank of America providing HR administration, payroll and timekeeping on its euHReka platform for 10 000 employees in Europe. ARINSO partnered with Accenture to provide the payroll aspects of the Unilever HRO deal.

## Xchanging

Xchanging grew out of the BaE shared services organisations, with venture capital funding. Xchanging focuses on customer services administration, finance and accounting, human resources and procurement outsourcing and has entered into joint venture arrangements with a number of its customers. Xchanging focuses on services to the insurance, financial services, manufacturing and retail sector. Its HR BPO experience is concentrated in the latter, where it delivers HR services to approximately 250 000 people and runs monthly payroll for a million people.

Xchanging's most significant recent deal was signed in summer 2005 with Boots. Under the 7 year, £400 million contract, Xchanging will manage travel expenditure, marketing, facilities management, resourcing and workplace services. The contract includes management of temporary labour supply.

## Capita

Capita is the number one BPO provider in the UK offering a comprehensive range of back office and front line services to the public and private sectors. Capita has a significant presence in service delivery in the UK public sector, including running the Congestion Charging scheme for Transport for London, the TV licensing scheme for the BBC and the Criminal Records Bureau for the Home Office.

In February 2006, Capita edged out Xchanging to capture a $245 million contract with the BBC covering the full range of HR administration and payroll services.

## Convergys

Convergys is a BPO provider providing customer care, billing and HR outsourcing services. A market leader in customer care, Convergys is growing its HRO capabilities and currently provides services to over 2 million employees per annum. In North America, it has been successful in capturing early market share in the public sector, notably a 2004 deal with the State of Florida to consolidate HR functions previously spread across 32 different agencies and to replace a 30-year-old IT platform with a leading edge web-based system.

Although it has no specific significant European only HRO contracts to date, in 2005 Convergys signed a US$240 million contract with the Whirlpool Corporation for payroll and staffing services which will cover the European workforce.

At the end of 2005 Convergys announced that it will provide comprehensive HR transactional services to DuPont's 60 000 employees and 102 000 retirees in 70 countries delivered in 30 languages around the world.

Convergys expects this contract to generate revenues in excess of US$1.1 billion over its 13-year duration. DuPont expects to realize a 20% productivity improvement as services transition to Convergys, increasing to 30% after 5 years.

**Xansa**

Xansa is a UK-based IT and outsourcing business whose public sector clients include the Department for Work and Pensions, HM Customs and Excise, Learning and Skills Council, NHS, Office of the Deputy Prime Minister, Office for National Statistics, Rural Payments Agency and Solihull Metropolitan Borough Council. In the private sector it has a contract to manage BT's payroll, finance and accounting and, in August 2006, announced a major deal with Lloyds TSB involving significant off shoring of back office administration, application support and general HR enquiry handling to India. As yet it still has to announce a significant full service HR outsourcing deal.

**Other potential players**

There are many other consultancies and systems integrators seeking to enter the HRO market. It is well known that CSC, for example, is very keen to sign their first full service HRO deal. CSC has recruited HRO professionals from Hewitts, Accenture, BT and Barclays Bank. CSC has also signed a global cooperation deal with AON to provide an end-to-end HRO capability offering.

## KEY TRENDS

The European HRO market appeared to falter in 2005, with no new transactions in Q1. However, things were picking up by the end of the year, with the Convergys/Whirlpool deal announced in July, followed by the Accenture/Bank of Ireland deal worth US$150 million in December. During 2005 and 2006 a period of necessary development of industry capabilities was seen to deal with the complexities of large scale HRO deals and it is predicted that 2007 will see a 17% increase in worldwide multi-process HRO.

Indeed, 2006 has seen this trend continue with strong growth across all market sectors with large deals involving the BBC, Centrica, IKEA and Lloyds TSB, all dwarfed by the US$1 billion contract between Accenture and Unilever, providing further evidence of substantial growth in Europe.

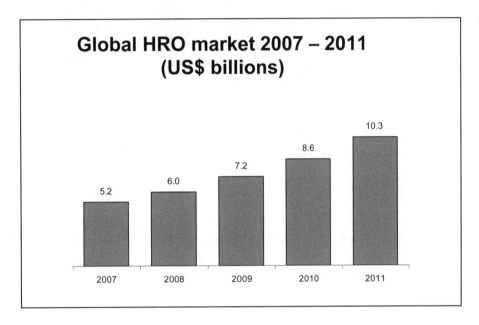

*Source: Orion Partners*

Average price per employee per year has fallen 53% since 1998 to approximately US$270 per head and it is predicted to continue to fall, as providers refine their delivery models and leverage offshore resources.

An increase in the number of 'multi-tower' BPO contracts, bundling HR with, for example, finance, accounting and procurement is also predicted. Bundling offers providers an opportunity for healthier margins and is a core strategy for some players, notably Accenture.

The US$ value of the global market is predicted to grow to almost US$100 billion by 2008 representing a 31% rise since 2005 with the Americas continuing to lead the way with growth of over 11% .The expansion of the market in Europe is also set to continue with growth of almost 8%.

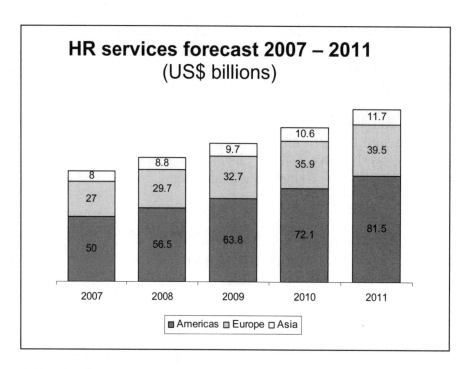

**Source: Orion Partners**

Recent deals in Europe, notably the Unilever and BBC contracts, are likely to have closed this forecast gap with the Americas (the IDC analysis was based upon 2005 data). What is clear is that all the leading providers are 'ramping up' their sales activity globally.

Regionally, growth in services shows a similar trend representing an increase in market share in the Americas from 59% to 60% with Europe losing ground from 32% to 31% over the same period. Growth in Asia is forecast to remain static.

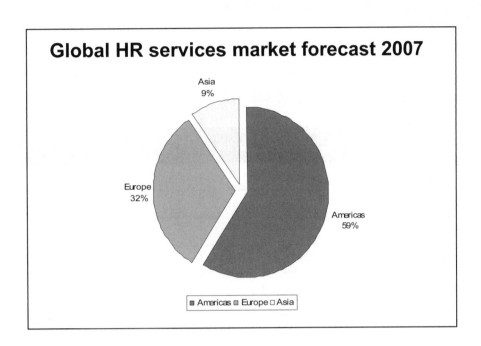

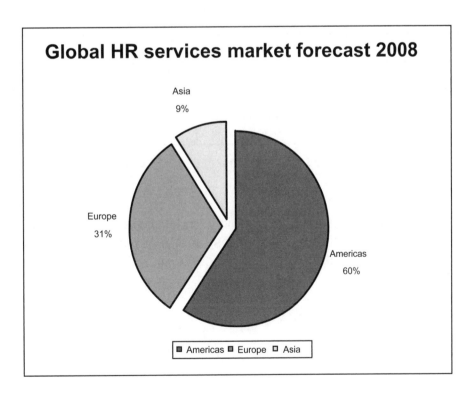

**Source: Orion Partners**

## SUPPLIER MARKET SHARE

Hewitt is dominant as the global market leader but Accenture leads in the European market. Many suppliers are still building their capabilities and there is persistent speculation regarding an Accenture/Hewitt merger. Whether or not this proves true, further market consolidation/purchase of specialist second tier benefits providers is anticipated.

### Leading Suppliers in European Market

|  | Number of transactions | Total contract value | Number of employees |
|---|---|---|---|
| Hewitt Associates | 9% | 12% | 6% |
| Accenture HR Services | 35% | 41% | 44% |
| Xchanging | 4% | 4% | 7% |
| EDS Corp | 9% | 19% | 22% |
| IBM Global Services | 9% | 3% | 1% |
| Capita | 4% | 4% | 2% |
| Northgate | 4% | 0% | 5% |
| LogicaKMG | 9% | 2% | 5% |
| Xansa | 4% | 5% | 5% |
| ARINSO | 4% | 1% | 1% |
| Agilisys | 4% | 5% | 1% |
| Fujitsu | 4% | 5% | 2% |
| **100%=** | **23 transactions** | **~$7 billion** | **~1.4 million employees** |

*Source: Orion Partners*

The top five providers for overall capability to deliver large-scale HRO, judged by global capability, offshore resources and size and breadth of current contract portfolio are (alphabetically) Accenture, ACS, Fidelity, Hewitt and IBM.

## PUBLIC SECTOR SPECIFIC DEALS

Although the UK public sector has embraced BPO in other areas, to date there have been relatively few public sector HRO deals concluded. Those that have been made are:

**Norfolk County Council:** In 1999 Norfolk signed a 10 year, £50 million deal with Capita to provide payroll and pensions. This was cancelled in 2003, only 4 years into the term, apparently a casualty of a change in the council's strategy. Both sides were at pains to emphasise that there were no service delivery issues, with Capita delivering 98.6% success against 70 performance targets in the final year.

**Thurrock Council:** Concluded a £427 million 15-year deal in 2004 with Vertex, the BPO arm of United Utilities plc, for a bundle of services including HR, procurement and finance and administration. As well as transferring 600 Thurrock employees and building a state-of-the-art business centre within the borough to house a new customer contact centre and provide accommodation for start-up businesses, Vertex has made a commitment to assist Thurrock's regeneration programme by creating 600 new jobs over the life of the contract.

**Metropolitan Police Authority:** In 2005 the Metropolitan Police Authority signed a deal with LogicaCMG for the provision of payroll and pensions administration services to the 46 000 officers and staff serving in the Metropolitan Police.

**Armed Forces Personnel and Administration Agency:** Entered a 10 year £600 million deal with EDS/ExcellerateHRO in 1998 for combined payroll, pensions and HR administration services to the Army, Navy and Air Force. (See Appendix B for a case study).

**Rochdale Metropolitan Borough Council:** Agreed an £200 million joint venture with Agilisys in April 2006. The services outsourced include HR and payroll, property management, highways and engineering, ICT and a contact centre. About 80 council staff will be seconded to Agilisys, apparently to give comfort regarding terms and conditions and pensions.

**Westminster City Council:** Multi-tower deal with a consortium led by Vertex, including HR services. (See Appendix B for a case study).

**Northern Ireland Dept. of Finance and Personnel:** Agreed a US$346 million contract with Fujitsu to modernize delivery of personnel services an eHR system as part of Civil Service reform in Northern Ireland. HR administration, payroll and recruitment are all covered by the deal.

# 4. INDICATIVE SCOPE OF SERVICES

The ideal scope of services for an HRO deal is a subject of some conjecture and forms the basis of significant discussion and negotiation between the customer and supplier. Research based on four deals indicates that HR services can be divided as into three groups; those that are frequently outsourced, those that are occasionally outsourced and those that are hardly ever outsourced. These three categories are summarized below.

At the heart of many of these deals is the outsourcing of HR systems and application management (SAP, Oracle, PeopleSoft and other specific tools) which are normally wrapped up as part of the overall service bundle. These services are excluded from this analysis which focuses on HR transactional and advisory services.

## *FREQUENTLY OUTSOURCED SERVICES INCLUDE:*

| Frequently outsourced services | |
|---|---|
| **Service line** | **Detailed activities** |
| **Recruiting (internal and external)** | ■ Sourcing candidates<br>■ Attracting candidates (inc. internal job posting)<br>■ Pre-screening<br>■ Campaign management<br>■ First interviews<br>■ Assessment testing<br>■ Assessment centre facilitation and delivery<br>■ All recruitment related administration (letters to candidates, setting up interviews, issuing rejections, candidate expense management)<br>■ Offer administration<br>■ Reference processing<br>■ On-boarding and induction administration<br>■ Pre-hire medicals |
| **Flexible (temporary) staffing** | ■ Selection and placement<br>■ Time reporting management<br>■ Invoicing management<br>■ Conversion to hire<br>■ Accounts payable |

Continued overleaf

Continued

| | Detailed activities |
|---|---|
| **Employee data/record management (status changes)** | <ul><li>Employee data record update</li><li>Maintenance of HRIS systems reporting hierarchies</li><li>Records/file maintenance (inc. document scanning)</li><li>Compliance and reporting</li></ul> |
| **Travel and expenses** | <ul><li>Expense claim processing</li><li>Expense record management</li><li>Reimbursement and cost allocation</li></ul> |
| **Payroll** | <ul><li>Time and attendance reporting and record management</li><li>On-cycle pay</li><li>Off-cycle pay</li><li>One-off payments and garnishments</li><li>Tax calculation and reporting</li><li>Disbursements</li><li>Accounting to general ledger</li><li>HM Revenue and Customs reporting</li><li>Year-end management (P11Ds, P60s etc)</li></ul> |
| **Benefits** | <ul><li>Enrolment and options administration management</li><li>Plan administration</li><li>Record maintenance</li><li>Claims administration</li><li>Third party management and liaison</li></ul> |
| **Compensation** | <ul><li>Salary administration</li><li>Bonus administration</li><li>Stock option administration</li><li>Savings plan administration</li><li>Total rewards statements</li><li>Elections/selection of flex benefits</li><li>Compensation job history records</li></ul> |
| **Performance management** | <ul><li>Performance review cycle administration</li><li>Absence monitoring</li><li>Absence management</li><li>Disciplinary and grievance record management</li></ul> |

Continued overleaf

Continued

| | Detailed activities |
|---|---|
| **Learning and development (including management development)** | ■ Development review process cycle administration<br>■ Learning plan maintenance<br>■ Catalogue maintenance<br>■ Demand management (scheduling)<br>■ Third party sourcing management<br>■ Delivery of training<br>■ Evaluation and assessment<br>■ Cost invoicing and allocation<br>■ Accounts receivable administration |
| **Relocation** | ■ Relocation query handling<br>■ Policy briefing and administration<br>■ Expenses processing and accounting<br>■ Inventory management<br>■ Relocation assistance (physical move support) |
| **Global postings/ mobility** | ■ Pre-departure administration and advice<br>■ On assignment support and administration<br>■ Visa and work permit administration<br>■ Repatriation management<br>■ Post repatriation support |
| **Exit** | ■ Exit administration<br>■ Voluntary exit administration<br>■ Involuntary exit administration<br>■ Exit data services (payroll and pensions data updates)<br>■ Redundancy and severance programme administration<br>■ Outplacement support |
| **Management reporting & surveys** | ■ General HR and management report support<br>■ Team and individual reports<br>■ Report writing services<br>■ Standard monthly reporting (balanced scorecard etc.)<br>■ Trend analysis<br>■ Surveys (inc. employee and Customer satisfaction) |
| **Vendor/third party management** | ■ Service management and reporting<br>■ Supplier sourcing and procurement<br>■ Invoicing and accounts |

Continued overleaf

Continued

| Frequently outsourced services Service line | Detailed activities |
|---|---|
| HR systems applications management | ■ See comment at the start of this section. HR systems platform implementation and management is usually outsourced as part of HRO deals |

## OCCASIONALLY OUTSOURCED SERVICES INCLUDE:

| Occasionally outsourced services Service line | Detailed activities |
|---|---|
| Recruiting (internal and external) | ■ Graduate recruitment activities<br>■ Senior management recruitment (specialized search agencies typically)<br>■ Executive recruitment (specialized search agencies typically)<br>■ Recruitment/resource planning |
| Compensation | ■ Executive compensation planning and administration<br>■ Reward policies and strategy |
| Performance management | ■ Interpretation of policy and practice around disciplinary and grievance processes<br>■ Industrial tribunal/legal support |
| Learning and development (including management development) | ■ Competency model development and maintenance<br>■ Standard training needs analysis<br>■ Career pathing and succession planning<br>■ Talent management administration<br>■ High-flier development programme design and delivery<br>■ Design of training solutions<br>■ Coaching and mentoring |
| Exit | ■ Exit interviews and analysis |

## RARELY OUTSOURCED SERVICES INCLUDE:

| Rarely outsourced services<br>Service line | Detailed activities |
|---|---|
| **Policy and strategy** | ▪ Corporate strategic planning, goal setting and forecasting<br>▪ HR policy development and design<br>▪ Legal compliance monitoring |
| **HR business partnering** | ▪ Strategic advice and support to business unit managers<br>▪ Business unit strategy and policy design |
| **Recruitment** | ▪ Authority to recruit<br>▪ Final interviews<br>▪ Selection decisions<br>▪ Offer package sign-off |
| **Employee relations** | ▪ Union/employee consultation and negotiation<br>▪ Collective bargaining activities |
| **Learning and development (including management development)** | ▪ Strategic training needs analysis<br>▪ Identification of high-fliers<br>▪ Talent management/executive succession planning |
| **Exit** | ▪ Exit/severance decisions |

A more detailed example of the transactional and advisory services from two major deals managed by a leading HRO provider is set out in Appendix C.

# 5. IMPLICATIONS FOR THE RETAINED HR FUNCTION

This section of the report examines the implications of HR outsourcing for the retained HR function. This is an area where, typically, insufficient attention to the impact of the outsourcing solution is given. This can seriously undermine the value of an outsourced-based service delivery HR model with the retained HR team unsure of their new role and resorting to double guessing and reworking the outputs of the outsource provider.

This section examines the impact on the retained HR function by exploring the implications of the following factors:

- **Design principles:** The implications of the design principles underpinning the scope and organizational design of the HRO solution need to be integrated with the strategic focus, services and scope of the retained function. Common agreement on service level requirements and measurements are key.

- **Service design options:** The extent to which services may be transferred to an outsource provider and the options available for transition to the new service.

- **Managing the relationship:** Ongoing considerations regarding governance structures as well as management and monitoring of the service need to be clearly established.

- **Skills requirements & future career pathing:** The capabilities required by the retained HR function are different to those operating in a non-HRO environment. There are also important implications in the career planning and pathing of development paths that need to be addressed.

## DESIGN PRINCIPLES

The most obvious starting point for any consideration of the HR outsourced model is the development of a common vision for the whole HR function, with a clear view of the strategic people priorities of the organisation. Ideally, this will be defined by the leadership team in conjunction with senior HR executives and will shape the scope of any proposed outsource.

What must be retained in-house to support competitive advantage and strategic thinking needs to be determined so that the scope of what can be placed with an outsource provider is confirmed. For example, talent management or the management of industrial relations are obvious areas that are likely to be fundamental to the success of a business and will most likely be retained. On the other hand the delivery of payroll services or the recruitment of standard high volume roles is likely to be ripe for outsourcing.

## SERVICE LED DESIGN

The new HR model design should be built with the concept of customer service at its heart. Ensuring that the service delivers on the key outputs that are required by the business is critical to achieving acceptance of the change.

This 'output' focus should be a key driver in determining the scope of what should be outsourced and what should remain in-house.

Similarly, a detailed definition of the roles and responsibilities within each of the key HR processes should be used to identify which activities require inputs and skills that are unique to the organisation, in contrast to those which are more generic and therefore readily available in the external market.

## DISCRETE VS EMBEDDED ACTIVITY

Another important distinction is between discrete and embedded processes. Discrete processes tend to be self-sufficient. They have dedicated resources (people, processes and systems) and few handoffs outside of a single team. For example, payroll is often set up as a discrete process, which is relatively easy to isolate and transition to an external provider.

Embedded processes are less well defined. Many resources are involved and there are many handoffs. For example, compensation administration is often 'embedded' in the sense that many parts of the HR function and the line are likely to be involved during the pay review cycle. A related issue is the range of separate systems that may provide data required to support the process and the complexity of the interfaces between them.

Discrete processes tend to fit the traditional BPO single service-line model whereas embedded processes can often only be addressed as part of a more extensive transformational approach to HR outsourcing which outsources the full 'back-office' service.

## RETAINED HR ORGANISATION DESIGN

A shared vision, based on business needs, helps shape the priorities. It should also be the key driver behind the design of the HR organisation. The typical approach to designing the HR delivery model is to categorize the activities of the HR function into three key groupings:

- Strategic – strategy & policy formulation;
- advisory – requires specific knowledge of the business, or application of commercial or professional judgement;
- transactional – high volume, standardized and repetitive.

In an in-house solution, these categories will drive the distinction between Group HR/Policy Centres of Excellence, business unit embedded HR Business Partner teams and Shared Services delivery.

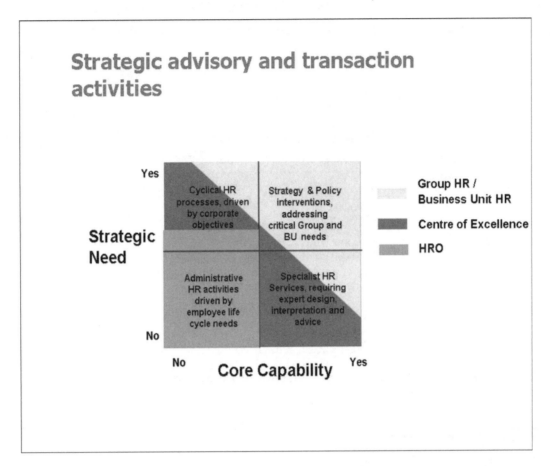

*Source: Reproduced with kind permission of Pinsent Masons*

The natural inclination can be to transfer the transactional shared service activity and retain the advisory and strategic support. However, an outsourced arrangement can also give a company access to economies of skill as well as scale in the more complex areas of HR service delivery. For example, an outsourced model has been proven to work very effectively in the areas of recruitment, performance management (grievance and disciplinary) and casework support, as long as the appropriate mechanisms are established to ensure that the retained organization has control over the quality of the service provided. In this case, the cut of activities suitable for outsourcing looks more like the diagram overleaf.

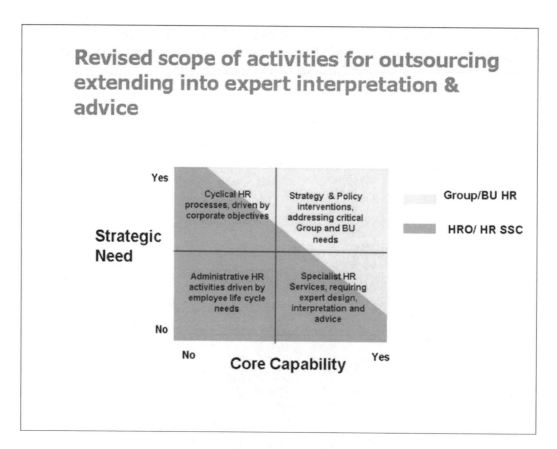

Revised scope of activities for outsourcing extending into expert interpretation & advice

| | | Group/BU HR |
| | | HRO/ HR SSC |

Strategic Need (Yes / No) vs Core Capability (No / Yes)

- Cyclical HR processes, driven by corporate objectives
- Strategy & Policy interventions, addressing critical Group and BU needs
- Administrative HR activities driven by employee life cycle needs
- Specialist HR Services, requiring expert design, interpretation and advice

*Source: Reproduced with kind permission of Pinsent Masons*

## DESIGN OPTIONS

The options for design and delivery of the service follow a continuum from a limited outsource of transactional activities through to a more comprehensive transfer of both transactional and advisory services. A hybrid model where different suppliers can be used for transactional and professional advisory services is another option. This may provide a more tailored solution, but can limit economies of scale and be more complex to manage.

The table on page 39–41 illustrates the options available and highlights the key factors to consider under each model. For each stage, the transfer of services to the outsourcer is increased and therefore the impact on the retained HR function is greater. No single deal in the market maps on to all aspects of 'stage 3' but the provision of these more sophisticated services is where the main suppliers are moving.

In summary, **stage 1** is the most basic HRO service where only the most transactional activity is in scope. This means that the retained HR function will be unlikely to be above, and often will be significantly below, a ration of 1 retained HR employee per 250 employees served (1:250). Therefore the retained HR function will still be heavily involved in the day-to-day query and routine management of HR services. In the private sector, the deal between BP and Exult (now Hewitt) most closely resembles this stage.

**Stage 2** is where the scope of services outsourced has cut significantly further into the retained HR functions area of responsibilities. Nearly all queries, including those involving policy interpretation and sensitive employee relations (disciplinary and grievance), have been outsourced. The ration of retained HR support to employees is 1:500. This stage is close to the scope of services provided under the Accenture/BT deal as it now stands.

**Stage 3** is the purist HR business partner (HRBP) and corporate centre of policy model where all non-core HR services have been outsourced. There are a number of deals in the market place (for example, IBM/P&G) which have elements of stage 3 in their contract design but no deal has yet been a pure 'stage 3' scope of services. The support ratios for the retained HR function are nearer to 1:1000+.

| Design Element | 'Stage 1' | Key Considerations | 'Stage 2' | Key Considerations | 'Stage 3' | Key Considerations |
|---|---|---|---|---|---|---|
| **Structure of service delivery** | Basic transactions outsourced, all advisory and BU specific support retained. | *Advantages*<br>■ *Perceived as lower risk.*<br><br>*Risks*<br>■ *Retained costs base is still high and limits BPO provider options for transformation of end to end delivery.*<br>■ *Retained staff 'over manage' provider and effort and costs are duplicated.*<br>■ *Line managers are confused as to who/how to access service.* | Transactions and basic caseworker support for recruitment, training and performance management outsourced.<br><br>Line managers receive most of their routine/day-to-day advisory services from the HRO provider teams. | *Advantages*<br>■ *Greater opportunities to transform processes and leverage vendor management capability.*<br>■ *Improved end-to-end MI as process managed within one entity.*<br><br>*Risks*<br>■ *Perceived loss of customer intimacy on more complex HR issues.*<br>■ *Retention of key organisational knowledge is more challenging.* | Contract management and lean HR BU team retained.<br><br>All additional activity, including specialist functional expertise outsourced. | *Advantages*<br>■ *Access at point of need, ultimate flexibility to access skills as required by organisation.*<br><br>*Risks*<br>■ *Lack of supplier management skills to leverage partnership effectively.*<br>■ *Loss of organisational knowledge.*<br>■ *Solutions insufficiently tailored.* |
| **Business embedded HR (HR business partners)** | Rarely involved in administration but often still the first point of contact for queries and requests. 35–45% of time on strategic/advisory issues. | *Advantages*<br>■ *Cost of basic administration is reduced and risk of loss of company knowledge mitigated.*<br><br>*Risks*<br>■ *Limited scope for retained HR to address higher value strategic issues and costs remain high.*<br>■ *Potential for duplication of effort.* | Provide a full 'business partner' service to their line managers. Do not handle queries re administration or data processing. Will offer support to the BPO provider on request in support of the case workers. Coach line to take responsibility for HR issues. | *Advantages*<br>■ *Retained HR released to fulfil more strategic role.*<br><br>*Risks*<br>■ *Potential for duplication and for retained staff to resort to case worker role.* | Lean in-house team with senior HR BP function providing as strategic support to BU leadership team. All routine HR activity provided through BPO transactional and caseworker teams. | *Advantages*<br>■ *Potential to maximize strategic HR capability.*<br><br>*Risks*<br>■ *Line manager buy-in to new approach.*<br>■ *Dilution of company specific support.*<br>■ *Skills mismatch of BP's to strategic roles.* |

Continued overleaf

Continued

| Design Element | 'Stage 1' | Key Considerations | 'Stage 2' | Key Considerations | 'Stage 3' | Key Considerations |
|---|---|---|---|---|---|---|
| **Policy and Centre of Excellence** | Pockets of excellence with deep knowledge of best practice and policy needs. | *Risks*<br>■ *May not cover all organisational requirements.*<br>■ *Limited control over cost or quality through fragmented approach.* | Formal CoE exist staffed by small team of recognized experts able to lead policy debates and support complex challenges and issues. Fragmented use of multiple external suppliers. | *Advantages*<br>■ *Greater access to external expertise.*<br>*Risks*<br>■ *Complex vendor management arrangements.* | Partnering with BPO provider to resource key external providers with greater depth and range of experience than in-house team could possess. Informed provider role for small core team in CoE's. | *Advantages*<br>■ *Greater access to external expertise.*<br>■ *Able to leverage buying power of BPO provider.*<br>*Risks*<br>■ *May limit independent access to 'best of breed'.* |
| **Service Channel Management** | Minimum employee and manager self service and outsourced helpdesk for basic HR queries. | *Advantages*<br>■ *Minimal investment costs and limited knowledge transfer requirements facilitate transition.*<br>*Risks*<br>■ *Limits leverage and requires higher retained headcount.* | eServices Technologies developed and introduced to enable managers to approve employee transactions, produce standard reports/ access basic team information, support pay review process and performance management.<br><br>Phone-based simple 'help desk' phone/email support available. Callers pointed to one telephone number/ email address. Staffs only have limited knowledge to answer simple questions. Simple IVR technology in place. Complexity causes callers to be passed on to in-house 'experts.' | *Advantages*<br>■ *Allows greater headcount consolidation.*<br>■ *Improve line manager decision making through better MI.*<br>*Risks*<br>■ *Line Mgr/employee acceptance of self-service reduces uptake.*<br>■ *Need to constantly refresh provider's knowledge base.* | eServices Sophisticated e-HR capability. All 'forms' can be completed on line and 80%+ of processes available on line. Sophisticated FAQs available to help customer. Full learning management system capability provides content and tools to desktop.<br><br>Phone-based insistence on one point of contact (email and/or phone) used for all queries. Knowledge based system supports BPO staff – guides them to answers. Skills based routing of calls/mails to knowledge experts. Use of call/email tracking and resolution via software. Rule | *Advantages*<br>■ *Customer experiences 'One stop shop' for majority of HR service requirements.*<br>*Risks*<br>■ *Relies on effective use of service performance MI for in-house team to interpret key people trends and challenges.*<br>■ *Committed line management support 'top to bottom' needed to embed change.* |

| Design Element | 'Stage 1' | Key Considerations | 'Stage 2' | Key Considerations | 'Stage 3' | Key Considerations |
|---|---|---|---|---|---|---|
| | | | Advice not offered. No issue resolution capability. | | based processes which can be fully or partially completed immediately. FAQs held on system to support first call/ email clearance of 80%+. Simple advice offered on most issues. Usage tracked and measured against SLAs. Issue resolution process in place. | |
| Technology | Ownership and maintenance of HRIS retained in-house. BPO provider only responsible for maintenance of data. | *Advantages*<br>■ *Full control of data set.*<br>*Risks*<br>■ *Full cost of technology and investment in maintenance and future upgrades retained in-house.* | Core HRIS managed and maintained by BPO provider. Additional 'tools on top' maintained by in-house specialists. | *Advantages*<br>■ *Ability to leverage technology BPO provider's investment in technology.*<br>*Risks*<br>■ *Integration may be complex with multiple interfaces.*<br>■ *Potential for data fragmentation increases complexity/cost of obtaining MI.* | BPO provider owns and maintains all HR technology and payroll applications. | *Advantages*<br>■ *Ability to leverage technology BPO provider's investment in technology.*<br>*Risks*<br>■ *Potential limit on flexibility.* |

## WHAT ADVISORY SERVICES SHOULD BE IN SCOPE?

A very common concern in clients looking to shape an effective HRO deal is to what depth should the contract include advisory services? Many HR professionals are very resistant to the thought of outsourcing detailed queries and policy interpretation to an external provider. However, in a number of areas there can be a very compelling case for outsourcing advisory services. At a generic level the outsourcing of advisory services can place the responsibility for managing the full scope of line and employee query handling under one roof. This can prevent unnecessary handoffs between the outsourcer and the retained HR function and assists in communicating to customers how to access services (for example, by allowing all transactional and advisory services to be accessed via one phone number and one email address). There are two main issues that support the outsourcing of advisory services. These are:

### 1. The depth of specialist knowledge required

The successful delivery of advisory services is dependent on the quality of the specialist advice behind the service. This is one area where an outsourcing partner can excel. It can be difficult, even for internal HR functions in large companies, to gain access to deep specialist knowledge and to constantly keep it up to date. Health and safety advice is a good example. The field is highly complex and driven by constantly changing legislation and case law. Outsource providers can afford the size of teams that are required to meet the depth and breadth of queries in this field. Furthermore, professionals in a specific field may even prefer to be part of a larger team of similar specialists, as this can offer enhanced career opportunities and encourage learning from peers. As a result this type of advisory work can be outsourced to good effect.

### 2. Ability to benefit from multi-client experience and infrastructure

Advisory services derive improved quality of service from access to information and infrastructure (for example, a sophisticated knowledge management decision support tool or customer relationship management (CRM) system) that an in-house HR function cannot often afford or support. Where this is the case, the argument for moving these services in scope becomes highly compelling.

## HR BUSINESS PARTNERS

The discussion above has highlighted the importance of the HRBP role. HR outsourcing will have huge implications for the HRBP role, especially if taken to the scope of services and implications spelt out above under the stage 3 type deals.

The table over the page summarizes how the HRBP role is usually shaped in response to the extent to which HR services have been passed to a third party.

| | Stage 1 | Stage 2 | Stage 3 |
|---|---|---|---|
| **HRBP role clarity** | HRBP role is differentiated from that of the HR generalist. Not involved in basic transactional work. Relations with line still based on reporting historic trends and some basic forecasting of requirements. Not invited to the strategy table by line or business unit leaders. Reports to overall HR Director who sets HRBPs objectives and carries out appraisals. Basic HRBP competencies defined. | HRBP role is clearly differentiated from role of Corporate or HQ strategy and policy team. No involvement in transactional work (which may be delivered via outsourcing or a shared service). HRBP performance objectives set by BU. Has place at the strategy table. Key focus is on developing BU tactics to deliver corporate objectives. Defines BU tactical HR strategy. Reports to BU CEO for objectives and appraisals. Dotted line to Group HRD. Fully fledged HRBP competency model defined and used in career pathing and talent management. | HRBP role focused on strategic support and guidance to the BU leadership. Same status and impact as other BU top team members. Leads cross functional change efforts. Expected to impact the bottom line by driving cost and efficiency initiates from the people angle. |
| **Professional, background experience and qualifications** | HRBPs have worked in at least one other function than HR. Will have higher degree/ qualification in HR related discipline. Regards HR as professional career. | Significant cross-sector and functional experience. Probably spent time in the line outside of the HR function. Business savvy. May have an MBA or equivalent. Commercially astute. Understands business drivers. Fully understands financial statements. | Business high-flier. Spends time in HRBP role as part of grooming for general management position. Will select HR career on basis that offers same rewards and challenges as other options. Fully rounded business-person. |
| **Orientation to the business** | HRBPs located with the business they support. Solid line reporting to HRD regarding objective setting and appraisal. HRBPs focus is split between traditional HR generalist responsibilities and some more strategic partnering activities. | HRBPs part of the BU leadership team. Only dotted line to HR functional leadership. HRBPs objectives set by BU leadership. Principal role is the tactical implementation of BU strategies. HRBPs not involved in HR administrative or transactional work. | HRBPs are the true 'voice of the business' on people related matters. Set own strategic agenda in discussion with BU CEO. Will have buyer/supplier relationship with HRSS and HR Centres of Excellence. |
| **Role as internal change consultant** | Will have a role to play in change projects. May lead a work stream or advise on impact of changes on HR policy. Provides expert advice on impact of employment laws on change proposals. Has 3–5 years experience of involvement in organisational change. Basic organisational development skills. | Recognized as a credible change consultant with broad range of transition management skills and experience. Will be expected to lead change projects and provide internal change advice as a viable alternative to hiring external consultants. Likely to have 7 years plus transition management experience. May well have worked as an external consultant previously. | Highly credible change leader. Has managed large complex transition programmes. May have international experience. Can influence and lead stakeholder groups. Able to challenge appropriately at the highest levels of the organisation. Fully rounded change agent skills. |

As well as the impact of outsourcing on the HRBP role, the arrival of an HRO deal also creates a number of new roles and challenges within the retained function. These new roles are primarily focused on measuring and managing the outsourced relationship and contractual arrangements.

## MANAGING THE RELATIONSHIP

One of the major impacts of the retained HR function is the requirement to manage the external Service Provider and to review service performance and issues requiring action in a regular and structured manner. This may result in the creation of new roles within the function such as 'Account Manager' and 'Service Analyst' to support the governance of the relationship.

### Governance

The management of the relationship between the retained HR function and the outsource provider needs to be focused on ensuring that the service disciplines are in place to deliver improved service quality and efficiency. The areas of focus should include:

- The continual translation of the business' strategy and requirements into a service that delivers those in the most innovative and efficient way;
- the management of the changes required in the service as business needs evolve over time (for example, volumes and service type);
- the measurement and reporting of service costs, performance and impact on the business, to allow performance evaluation and for improvement targets to be set.

A dedicated account team would typically be established to work jointly to understand the business strategy and objectives. In doing so, they would agree how the HRO provider would contribute to the achievement of these objectives.

This team would typically agree metrics to track that impact and bring the benefits of the new operating model. The outsourcer should be incentivized to deploy their resources in the most innovative and effective way in the delivery of the service. Annual service plans for each business unit would typically need to be agreed with the HRO Account Manager and documented in an Account Plan.

Ideally the team would work together informed by common values that would include:

- The sharing of financial and business objectives and other appropriate information;
- the joint ownership of service improvement and continuous improvement;
- leveraging the combined capabilities of both organisations to deliver an enhanced service;
- striking the appropriate balance between cost and quality.

### Key Service Forums

A number of formal forums would need to be established to ensure open communications with stakeholders. These provide a formal framework within which the informal and more regular contacts at every level operate. They provide a clearly defined route for the escalation of issues and the review of service performance.

Typical forums would include:

### Quarterly Joint Review Board

This group brings together the senior client users (HR and business representatives), and the joint account teams. This forum is typically used to agree the strategic focus and performance levels, agree and review financial performance and to explore and discuss critical incidents.

### Monthly Business Unit Reviews

These forums bring together the relevant Account Manager, the Head of Service Operations from the HRO provider, the HRO Process Owners (Service Line Heads) as required, Business Unit HR and business representatives. Their purpose is to review service change requests to ensure they are aligned with BU strategies, review financial performance and forecast volumes, review service performance and agree action plans and review high-priority incidents.

### HR Forums

Bi-monthly reviews where HRO Service Line Heads and key functional leads meet to review key aspects of functional HR strategy and delivery – for example, resourcing or reward.

## NEW ROLES, SKILLS AND CAREER PATHING

### Contract and Service Management

Many HR professionals will have had the experience of managing external providers in individual contracts, although some will have relied heavily on procurement specialists to provide contract management expertise. The transition to managing a set of service outputs rather than process inputs will be a challenge for many retained HR staff and will require a different mindset and approach. It is likely that the team with primary responsibility for managing a HRO supplier will require the development of commercial skills in the areas of negotiation, analysis and issue resolution and performance tracking.

### Improved Business Planning

The buyer/supplier disciplines that begin to be embedded in an internal shared services function take on a greater significance within a commercial outsource arrangement. The mechanisms for defining the volumes of a particular type of service required need to be more precise and the consequences of inaccurate planning can be costly. Contracts can be structured to provide flexibility, but flexibility will typically come at a cost, as it will restrict the provider's ability to flex their resource if peaks and troughs in demand are not planned.

The implications for the retained HR function are more fundamental than the need for the contract management disciplines outlined above. For the function to become an 'intelligent client' that can drive maximum benefit from an external provider, they will need to ensure that business HR teams form an integral part of the core business planning processes. Early visibility of the people management implications of changes to business plans will enable a better forecasting of demand. In due course this will allow a higher quality of service provision and greater predictability of cost.

### Internal Consultancy Skills

As outlined above, the shift in emphasis in the business partner role will be from technical expert to business generalist and strategist. The outcomes expected of the successful business partner will be more akin to those of an internal consultant.

These would include relationship building, diagnosis, solution shaping and so on. This is then underpinned by a deep 'spike' of content skills that the BP would bring to bear in their specific area of expertise, be it business unit or functionally based. The important point to make here is that in the context of a HRO delivery model, the key is for HR Business Partners to know how to access technical expertise rather – knowing what you don't know, and knowing someone who does.

### Career Pathing and Career Management

The traditional career model for HR has already changed significantly with the introduction of shared services. The route from administrative expert through functional specialist or HR generalist has needed to be revisited.

Post HRO, the vast majority of HR technical administrative skills will reside outside the organisation with the third party provider. Consequently the old career paths will have been removed and new internal career pathing is required. One solution that is emerging is that organisations are seeking to ensure that provisions are made to facilitate transfers and secondments from the outsourcer to the retained function and vice versa to ensure the full breadth of professional development opportunities are available.

# 6. CONTRACTUAL OPTIONS

This section of the report summarizes the seven most common contractual options for structuring the outsourced relationship.

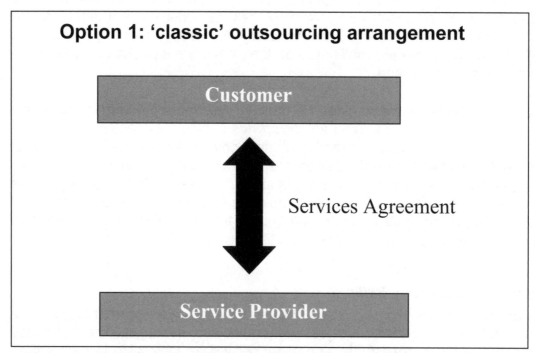

**Option 1: 'classic' outsourcing arrangement**

*Source: Reproduced with kind permission of Pinsent Masons*

This is the 'classic' outsourcing arrangement to a single Service Provider. The customer enters into a Services Agreement with the Service Provider under which Service Provider provides services for a fee. Any of the customer's employees who are assigned to provide the services outsourced will transfer under TUPE.

The fee structure may include an element of risk/reward, for example a share of any cost savings realized or penalties for failure to meet agreed service levels.

The advantage of an arrangement with a single Service Provider is straightforward, arm's length and well understood. There is a single managerial interface and a single point of responsibility.

Disadvantages include dependence on a single source which may expose the customer to loss, for example, if the Service Provider becomes insolvent. Further, while this structure was most used for the earliest outsourcing contracts for simple services such as cleaning and security, in the case of more complex HRO, the Service Provider may not have the internal competence or resources to manage the complexities and cover all the customer's requirements.

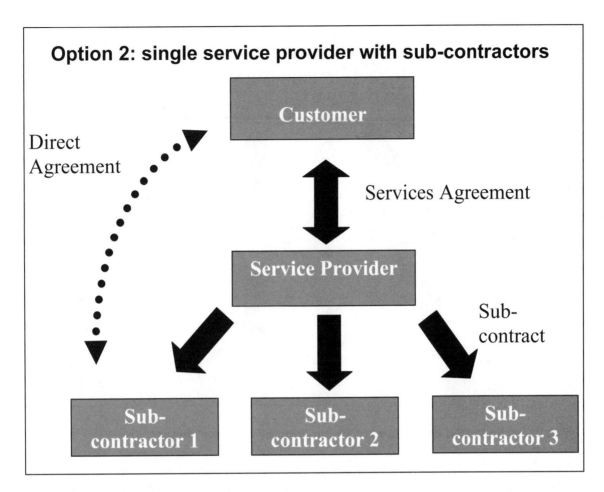

**Option 2: single service provider with sub-contractors**

Customer

Direct Agreement

Services Agreement

Service Provider

Sub-contract

Sub-contractor 1

Sub-contractor 2

Sub-contractor 3

*Source: Reproduced with kind permission of Pinsent Masons*

On the customer side, this structure is the same as option 1, with a Services Agreement with a single Service Provider. The Service Provider however engages a number of sub-contractors to provide any additional skills and capacity the Service Provider lacks to deliver the services.

Where one sub-contractor is particularly significant, for example, because it provides a material part of the service, the customer may also enter a direct agreement with that sub-contractor, allowing the customer to step-in to the sub-contract should the Service Provider become insolvent or otherwise fail (shown with a dotted line above). The customer would normally only do this on a temporary basis (that is, while it found a new primary Service Provider) although occasionally the sub-contractor is so substantial that it is capable of taking over the whole prime contract itself.

The advantages and disadvantages are similar to option 1 although somewhat mitigated by the Service Provider's ability to plug gaps in its own expertise and resources with sub-contractors. A direct agreement with key sub-contractors may give a degree of protection to the customer in the event of failure of the prime Service Provider.

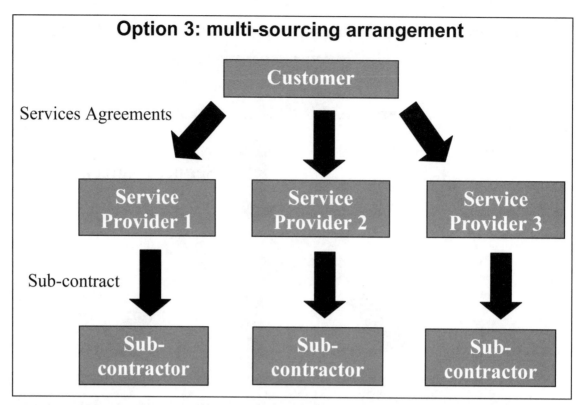

**Option 3: multi-sourcing arrangement**

Customer

Services Agreements

Service Provider 1

Service Provider 2

Service Provider 3

Sub-contract

Sub-contractor

Sub-contractor

Sub-contractor

*Source: Reproduced with kind permission of Pinsent Masons*

Option 3 is a multi-sourcing arrangement under which the customer acquires services from a number of Service Providers, normally on the basis that each is specialist in a particular area, for example, pensions, payroll and training.

The customer will enter into Service Agreements with each of the Service Providers. In each contract it will specify that the Service Provider in question has to cooperate with the other Service Providers but the burden of enforcing that cooperation will ultimately lie with the customer. Some customers have attempted to overcome this by requiring the various Service Providers to enter into contracts or service level agreements directly with each other, specifying how they will cooperate with each other, but in practice this has proved to have limited effectiveness.

The main advantage of this structure is that the customer can choose the best in class in the various areas of expertise rather than relying on a single Service Provider. It may also make transition easier to manage as the Service Agreements can be entered into sequentially, allowing time to bed down one element before transition of the next commences. In addition, because there will normally be some overlap in competence, the customer may have a fall-back position if one of the Service Providers fails: The scope covered by that Service Provider can often be reassigned to one or more of the remaining Service Providers – at least on a temporary basis.

The primary disadvantage of this approach is increased cost for the customer in managing three (or more) interfaces rather than one. Establishing accountability in case of failures can also be difficult as the Service Providers have a tendency to blame each other for failures.

---

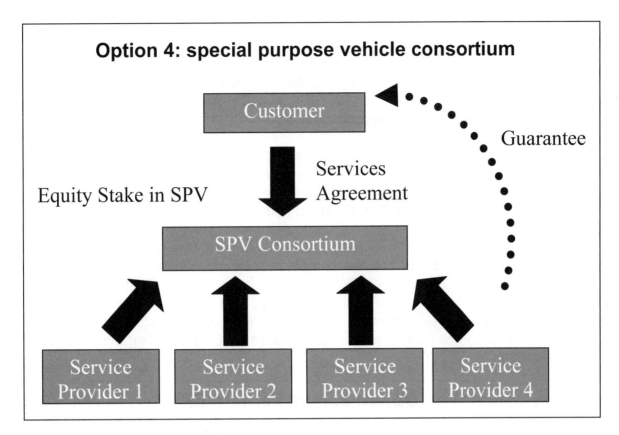

**Source: Reproduced with kind permission of Pinsent Masons**

Option 4 is designed to overcome the problem of managing multiple supplier relationships illustrated in option 3, by requiring the Service Providers to form a consortium of some sort. The customer then enters into a Services Agreement with the consortium.

The consortium can take the form of a separate company in which all the Service Providers are shareholders, in which case the customer may well require guarantees of that company's performance from the individual Service Providers – as shown for Service Provider 4 in the above diagram. Alternatively, the vehicle for the consortium may be a partnership or contractual joint venture, in which case all the individual Service Providers will be jointly and severally liable to the customer so no additional guarantee is necessary.

There will be various agreements between the Service Providers themselves (depending on the form of the consortium) but these do not directly involve the customer. There may also be individual services agreements between the consortium and the Service Providers, particularly where the consortium takes the form of an SPV company, but again, these are part of the internal management of the consortium and do not involve the customer.

Advantages for the customer are access to a broader range of expertise offered by multiple Service Providers, with the benefit of a single interface – even in the case of a contractual joint venture the Services Agreement will normally require the Service Providers to present a single managerial interface to the customer. As well as reducing management cost for the customer in case of service failure, all of the Service Providers are responsible to the customer for failure at the consortium level. The customer can therefore focus on agreeing remedies for failure with the consortium and leave the Service Providers to sort out between themselves how any additional cost should be apportioned.

Although it simplifies things for the customer, the consortium structure imposes additional expense and overhead upon the Service Providers, as well as the potential risk of being responsible for each others failures. The cost of these elements will be reflected in the price.

Where the rewards of the individual service elements are high enough, and no single Service Provider has the competence or resources to take on the role of prime contractor, Service Providers will form consortia – it is a common structure for large public-sector contracts. However where one Service Provider is a natural candidate for the role of prime contractor, the customer can often achieve similar advantages, at less cost, by adopting either option 1 or option 2.

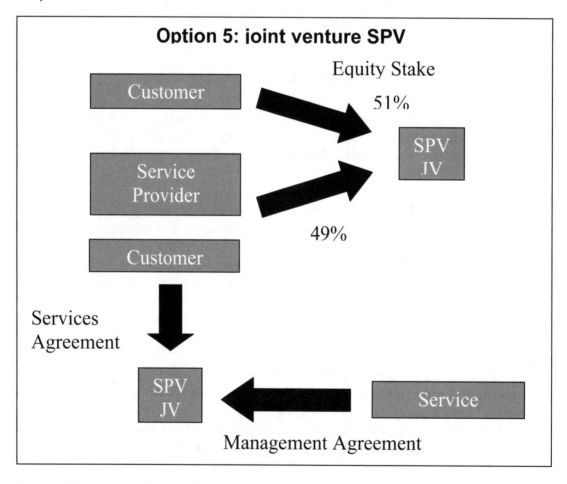

**Source: Reproduced with kind permission of Pinsent Masons**

In this structure, the customer and Service Provider form a special purpose vehicle joint venture company. The equity division of 51%/49% shown in the illustration is the most common, as the joint venture company remains a subsidiary of the customer it forms part of the same group for VAT purposes.

The customer then enters into a Services Agreement with the joint venture company. Because the services are provided to the customer by a subsidiary they do not attract VAT. However, many of the required services (for example, management expertise and use of hardware and software) will have to be sourced by the joint venture company from the Service Provider and the agreement for the provision of those services to the joint venture company will attract VAT. Therefore, the amount of VAT that is saved by this arrangement normally equates to the VAT on the labour element provided by employees of the joint venture company.

The main advantage of this structure is the potential VAT saving described above. However, this is normally only of significance where the customer does not charge VAT on the whole or a substantial part of its own activities and cannot make full recovery of VAT.

Unless VAT is a consideration, the disadvantages of this structure may point to other structures being more suitable. In addition to considerable contractual complexity, if there is a failure in the provision of services to the customer, primary responsibility lies with the joint venture company, which is a subsidiary of the customer. The customer is thus prima facie responsible for 51% of the resulting loss. While the joint venture company will attempt to transfer responsibility for 100% of the loss to the Service Provider under its Management Agreement, the inherent complexity of the arrangement imposes a significant management overhead.

It is likely that option 5 is highly attractive as a way of structuring any HRO deal. Partly this is because of the VAT issue, but it is also because it allows the customer to retain a large measure of control over the HRO deal during the transition and transformation period. Consequently, it allows the customer to keep their options open so that they can decide to sell or float the joint venture vehicle or bring the service back fully in-house if strategic priorities change.

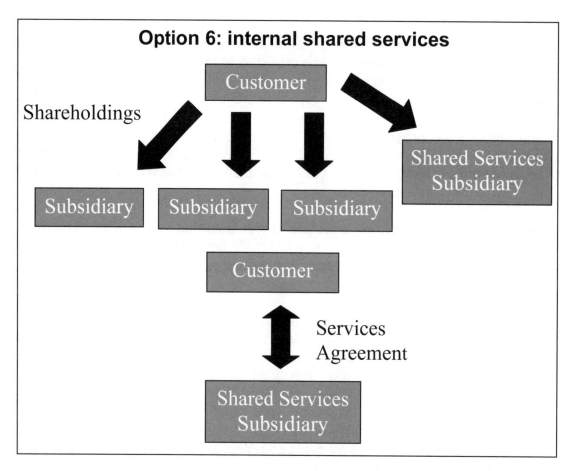

**Option 6: internal shared services**

Shareholdings

Customer

Subsidiary    Subsidiary    Subsidiary

Shared Services Subsidiary

Customer

Services Agreement

Shared Services Subsidiary

*Source: Reproduced with kind permission of Pinsent Masons*

Option 6 addresses the internal structure of service provision in the customer. In groups of companies it is not uncommon for each subsidiary to have its own separate IT, procurement, HR or other function. Equally, in many companies, such functions are grouped in a services company (a 'Shared Services Subsidiary') – a company whose role is to provide those functions to all the other companies in the group.

We have only shown a Services Agreement between the Shared Services Subsidiary and the holding company (assuming that to be the customer) but there can be as many Services Agreements as there are subsidiaries and they can take the guise of formal contracts or informal Service Level Agreements depending on various tax and other considerations.

The Shared Services Subsidiary may either provide services from its own resources or purchase them from an external Service Provider – in which case it becomes the 'customer' in whichever of Structures 1–5 applies, with the same advantages and disadvantages that attach to each structure.

Some organisations have succeeded in turning their own shared services arrangements into Service Providers serving the external market, for example Xchanging.

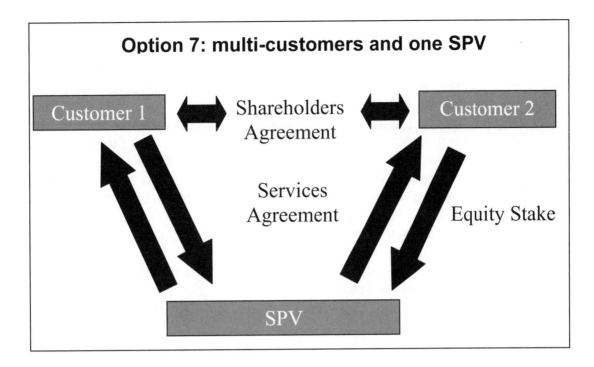

*Source: Reproduced with kind permission of Pinsent Masons*

The structures in options 1–6 have assumed a single customer (whether a single company or a group of companies). This structure covers the situation where there is more than one customer. It could be described as an External Shared Services Structure (as opposed to the Internal Shared Services Structure shown in structure 6).

Under this structure, two customers set up a shared services company as a special purpose, joint venture vehicle and outsource one or more services to it. For example, certain banks have outsourced their cheque processing services in this way. Each customer's investment in the joint venture company is dealt with through the Memorandum and Articles of the joint venture company and the relationship between them, as shareholders, will normally be dealt with in a shareholders agreement. The joint venture company then enters into a Services Agreement with each of the customers.

As with Structure 5, the fact that each customer has an equity stake in the SPV requires some care in managing the conflicting interests of the customers as investors, managers and service recipients and means that the question of liability is complex. As with Structure 6, the SPV may provide the services itself or use an external Service Provider to do so, in which case any of Structures 1–5 might apply to the relationship between the SPV (as customer) and the Service Provider. The most complex position is reached where the external Service Provider itself takes an equity stake in the SPV (an arrangement that is used in one of the cheque processing outsourcings).

The advantages of this structure lie in the economies of scale and standardisation of processes. In the case of cheque processing, for example, the decline in the use of cheques made it increasingly uneconomic for a single bank to maintain the necessary infrastructure and a shared (and standardized) solution was more appropriate. In the example where the Service Provider took an equity stake, the intention was to sell the solution to further banks so as to maintain volumes at an acceptable level. By taking a majority stake the parties were able to portray the SPV to an eligible bank as a subsidiary of the Service Provider rather than of two of the bank's rivals.

The disadvantage of this type of structure is its complexity and in practice terms it has proved difficult (despite Service Provider equity stakes) to sell the solution to any customer except the founding customers, which may threaten the long-term viability of the solution.

# 7. ENGAGEMENT AND TRANSITION

Planning and managing the transition of the service from in-house ownership to the outsourcing partner's control is one of the most demanding and intensive parts of the outsourcing process. It is also an opportunity to set the tone and future success of the outsourcing contract. This chapter examines the main aspects of transition and the key success criteria for achieving lasting benefits.

The transition phase should be managed as a clearly defined stage in the execution of the HRO contract's implementation. It should seek to achieve four objectives:

- Agree the contract for services;
- transfer operational responsibility for the service and manage the stabilisation process;
- transfer staff to the Service Provider and establish the service delivery team;
- establish the IT infrastructure on which the service will initially operate.

Below are outlined the key elements of the transition process and the associated risks that need to be addressed.

## TRANSITION PLANNING

The diagram below sets out a high level example of the typical work streams that need to be in place during the transition phase.

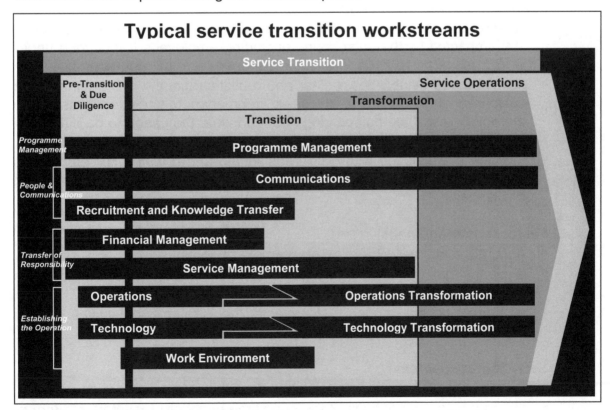

*Source: Orion Partners*

---

The graphic on the previous page shows the various work streams of activities cutting across four stages of the transition. Namely:

- The initial pre-transition and due-diligence phase (this is typically 3–4 months in duration);
- the core transition period (4–6 months) where services are cut over to the new provider;
- the transformation period (6–18 months) where the provider consolidates, stabilises and begins to significantly improve the effectiveness of transferred processes;
- service operations which represent the day-to-day management of service delivery once transition has been completed and achieving stability of process operations is the principle focus.

Successful transitions will normally require the presence of the following work streams and activities:

### Programme management
- A clearly articulated vision and scope for the delivery of services;
- experienced project management capability and controls to manage multiple work streams;
- a clear benefits delivery plan which spells out what benefits will be (should have been) delivered by a particular date;
- a clearly defined governance structure that represents the business (that is, HR's customers) interests.

### People and communications
- Responsible for managing the change and transition issues as they affect staff impacted by the outsourcing (including employees transferring under TUPE, the retained HR operation, line managers and employees.
- develops and establishes a clear and realistic rationale in the mind of the customers of the service (employees, line managers and executives), as to the objectives of the outsourcing deal and what they need to do differently in order to access services under the new arrangements;
- manage the dialogue with both transitioning and retained HR employees as to the purpose of the change as well as associated opportunities and challenges.

### Financial management
- Accurate and timely control of programme budgets;
- a clearly defined and regularly reviewed business case and benefits delivery plan for the outsourcing deal;
- a simple pricing model that reflects the strategic objectives of the outsourcing relationship.

### Service management
- A set of baseline service measures and costs tracked over time;
- the contractual obligations of the outsource provider presented in a format that the retained HR team can easily refer to and understand;

- understanding of the service provided and how retained HR and business managers can engage effectively to deliver its objectives;
- regular service reporting, reviews and well established service governance relationships;
- clear business readiness processes to ensure that HR customer's are fully briefed on the impact of the deal and have prepared for the changes ahead of go-live dates.

### Operations transfer

- A transfer of operational knowledge (both tacit and explicit) required to operate and run the service. This may include; HR supplier relationships, business unit 'political' awareness and detailed current process knowledge;
- the development within the supplier of a cultural awareness of the client's organisation.

### Technology transfer

- Integration with service design and development of business requirements;
- cleansing and transfer of data to the provider's systems;
- data collection for new data;
- accurate mapping and development of existing interfaces;
- developing a stable technology platform on which to deliver the service.

# FACTORS INFLUENCING THE TRANSITION APPROACH

Each organisation's approach to transition will be unique within the context of the deal structure, organisational context and culture and transformation agenda. The high-level transition plan example over the page provides a generic view of the approach taken for a multi-site, single country transition. This is an aggressive timeline that probably represents the minimum time in which this process could be completed for a large scale organisation. The initial Transition of Services Plan shown over page is achieved in a 3 month period with service stabilisation, 'quick win' improvements and fully fledged service reporting implemented within a further 6 months. In Orion's experience the quickest possible time to begin and end transition is around 9 months with the majority of deals taking 12–18 months and with a handful of notorious ones that have lasted longer than 24 months.

# Three month initial transition activities

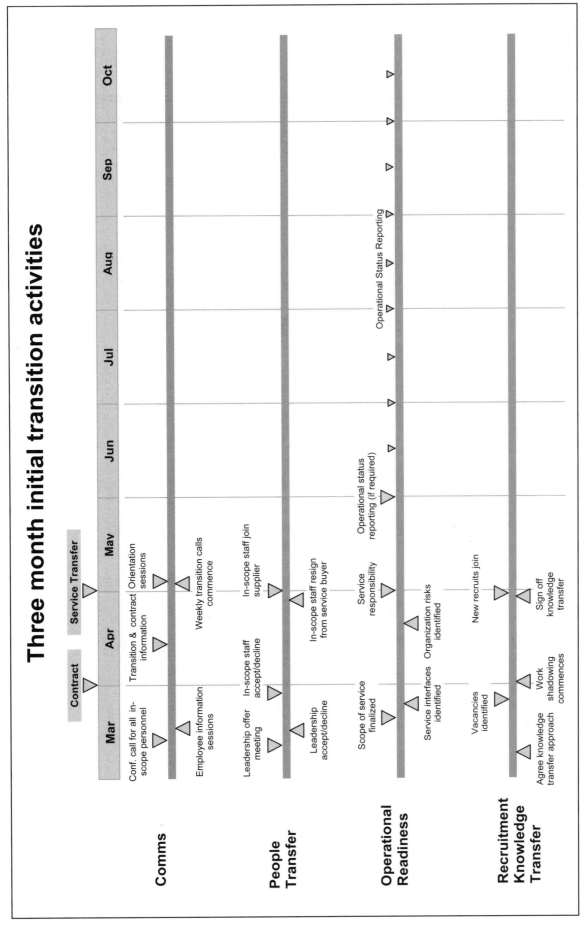

**Source: Orion Partners**

# Stabilisation and initial transformation activities

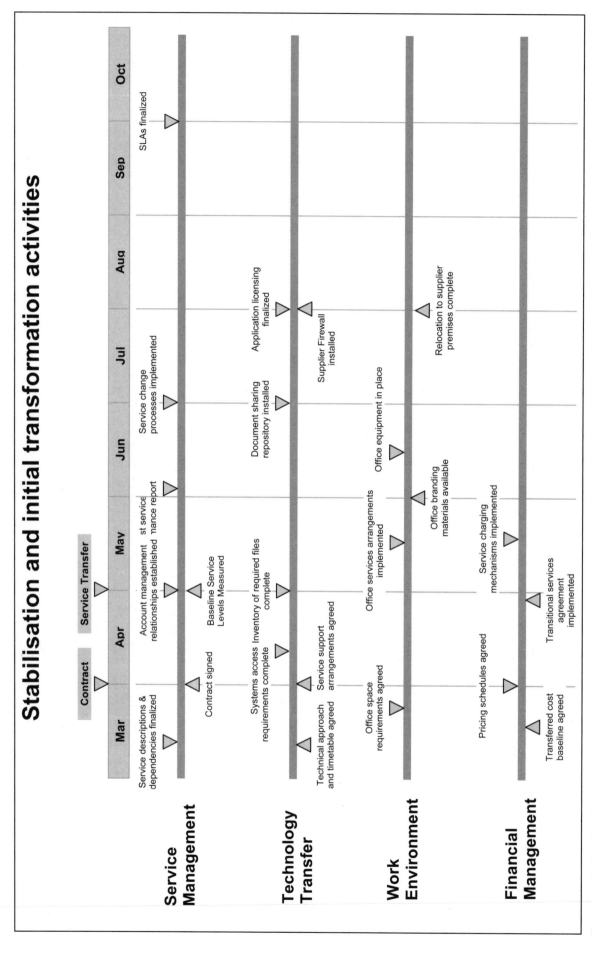

**Source: Orion Partners**

In developing the generic transition model, there are a number of factors that influence the timing and activities found within the detailed plan:

### Transition and transformation
The traditional approach to HRO transition has often been one summarized as 'lift and shift'. The current processes, people and technologies are moved, unchanged, to the supplier's control. It offers a low risk approach and minimizes the amount of change occurring at a high risk time.

However, in some circumstances, it may be necessary to undertake transformation activities prior to or immediately after the transition, for a variety of reasons:

- It may be necessary to move processes delivered at multiple locations onto new IT platforms to consolidate them at the supplier's delivery locations.
- The business case may demand early delivery of benefits from transformation, thus requiring a curtailed transition period and focus on transformation as early as possible.
- Some standard, straightforward and discrete processes may be simple to move to the supplier's delivery model and hence deliver an early 'quick win'.

In each instance, the case for undertaking transition and transformation activities must be considered against the risk profile of the programme overall. In the vast majority of HRO deals, transformation activities happen 6–18 months after the transition has been achieved and the service has been given time to embed in under the new management.

### Geographical relocation of the transferring operations
The extent to which the location of the delivery of services is different from the previous location will drive the complexity of the transition planning. For example, the scale, complexity and timing of a transition to a new service on a greenfield (new) site will be significantly different from the more straightforward transfer of existing facilities to a supplier.

Specifically, the time taken to acquire and 'fit out' the new site will delay the delivery of benefits and, consequently, drive up transition cost and risk. The further the location is away from the current location then the less likely it is that experienced staff will transfer to the new Service Provider. This augments the effort needed to capture knowledge ahead of service migration.

### Service scope
The scope of the service being outsourced will be a significant influencing factor on the approach and plan for the transition phase. The need to reduce the risk of service failure can determine specific transition approaches for individual process areas.

For example, activities like payroll, which whilst discrete in nature are (potentially) high-profile failure risks if the monthly cycle is disrupted and staff miss salary payments. To minimize the risk of a highly visible service failure it may necessitate the outsourcer deciding to take control of the process *in situ* and stabilise this under the new management team. Only then will the process migrate to the supplier's environment and location. The transition of operational ownership for these processes may also be delayed until lower risk processes have been completed and confirmed a success.

## *EXAMPLE TRANSITION RESPONSIBILITIES*

Transition is a demanding time for the client organisation. A failure to acknowledge or prepare for the demands placed on the company will potentially be detrimental to the contract's success and the financial success of the relationship. Outlined below are the key responsibilities of each party in the transition phase.

Suppliers should have access to the capabilities and resources to meet these needs and will typically retain experienced teams to undertake these activities. The need to maintain business-as-usual activities coupled with the specialist nature of transition tasks will often force an organisation to seek external support to tackle the changes.

| Transition Activities | Service Provider | Client |
|---|---|---|
| Account (relationship) management | ■ Appoint Account Director.<br>■ Account Director to attend Programme Steering Committee meetings.<br>■ Lead preparation of contract schedules and negotiation. | ■ Appoint Service Director/Manager.<br>■ Service Director/Manager to attend Programme Steering Committee meetings.<br>■ Lead preparation of contract schedules and negotiation. |
| Transition programme management | ■ Appoint Implementation Programme Manager.<br>■ Manage and own programme budget and progress tracking.<br>■ Report to Steering Committee on programme budget and progress.<br>■ Track and agree all changes to programme scope, business case and budget.<br>■ Agree acceptance criteria and manage process, including actions to ensure criteria are met.<br>■ Sign-off contract schedules (executive accountability). | ■ Appoint Implementation Programme Manager.<br>■ Appoint Steering Committee members (Senior HR and Business Representatives).<br>■ Sign-off all changes to programme scope and budget.<br>■ Agree acceptance criteria.<br>■ Sign-off business case and acceptance criteria as met.<br>■ Sign-off contract schedules (executive accountability). |
| People and communications | ■ Define and execute communications strategy and plan.<br>■ Develop retention and key people plan.<br>■ Manage staff transfer and induction.<br>■ Staff recruitment.<br>■ Complete supplier communications. | ■ Agree stakeholder groups.<br>■ Define and execute communications strategy and plan.<br>■ Sign-off overall communications strategy and plan.<br>■ Sign-off retention and key people plan.<br>■ Complete supplier communications. |

| Transition Activities | Service Provider | Client |
|---|---|---|
| IT implementation | <ul><li>Manage design process – complete design specifications.</li><li>Manage system build and configuration.</li><li>Unit and system testing.</li><li>Application integration.</li><li>Define and execute data migration.</li></ul> | <ul><li>Define business process requirements.</li><li>Review and agree design specifications.</li><li>Define security, IT, networking and integration standards.</li><li>Sign-off data migration plan.</li><li>Provide mapping for data migration.</li><li>Complete user testing of functionality, interfaces and data migration.</li><li>Facilitate interaction with outgoing suppliers.</li></ul> |
| Operational implementation | <ul><li>Appoint service delivery team.</li><li>Complete process mapping.</li><li>Complete local work instructions.</li><li>Complete delivery team training (IT, process and cultural).</li><li>Input to services schedule of the contract.</li><li>Migrate supplier contracts.</li><li>Prepare contingency planning.</li><li>Participate in User Acceptance Testing.</li></ul> | <ul><li>Appoint day-to-day operational points of contact.</li><li>Confirm TUPE position of current staff.</li><li>Sign-off knowledge capture.</li><li>Agree final processes.</li><li>Input to services schedule of the contract.</li><li>Provide cultural orientation training for new supplier staff.</li><li>Sign-off IT functional specification, including reporting.</li><li>Provide authorisation policies.</li><li>Identify all business and HR users.</li><li>Prepare contingency planning.</li><li>Participate in User Acceptance Testing.</li></ul> |
| Work environment | <ul><li>Define work environment requirements for client site if necessary (desk space and IT desktop, postal services, telephony).</li><li>Review Health and Safety requirements at client site.</li><li>Establish work environment at Service Provider's sites.</li></ul> | <ul><li>Agree, provide and maintain work environment to agreed specification.</li><li>Agree, provide and maintain IT desktop and telephony infrastructure to agreed specification.</li></ul> |
| Service management | <ul><li>Agree final Service Management Framework.</li><li>Manage base lining and reporting processes.</li><li>Prepare final contracts.</li><li>Establish initial Account Management meetings.</li><li>Establish continuous improvement process.</li></ul> | <ul><li>Provide historical benchmark data for Key Performance Indicators (KPIs) and Service Level Agreements (SLAs).</li><li>Provide required input data for base lining SLAs and Operating Level Agreements (OLAs or reverse SLAs).</li><li>Sign-off KPIs, SLA and OLA targets.</li><li>Prepare final contracts.</li><li>Agree final Service Management Framework.</li></ul> |
| Financial management | <ul><li>Validate financial assumptions.</li><li>Provide Sales Ledger contact for billing queries.</li><li>Input to pricing and billing schedules.</li><li>Establish billing processes to client-billing requirements.</li></ul> | <ul><li>Provide data as required to validate financial assumptions.</li><li>Provide Finance team contact for Purchase Ledger queries.</li><li>Input to pricing and billing schedules.</li><li>Provide billing back-up data requirements.</li><li>Agree invoicing requirements (within commercial terms).</li></ul> |

## TRANSITION RISKS

The transition phase undoubtedly represents a period of high risk. Nonetheless, the key risks are well recognized and can be managed. The common risk areas are reviewed below alongside potential mitigation strategies.

| Risk | Detail | Mitigation |
|------|--------|------------|
| Limited commercial experience of functional staff involved in the contract negotiation, leading to a poor contract for the service buyer. | The development of the contract schedules for service and pricing, in particular, will require significant input from staff with a detailed knowledge of the current processes and services. These staff are typically drawn from middle and junior management levels of the HR organisations and are often unused to commercial negotiation.<br><br>The outsourcing supplier will deploy staff who are more experienced in this area to work with them. This will leave the in-house team at a disadvantage as the detailed schedules are developed. | Staff need a clear negotiating framework within which to work. This should include:<br>■ Example acceptable service definitions (including target service levels);<br>■ target service cost, by process area if necessary;<br>■ internal review and sign off processes for each piece of work;<br>■ rules of engagement with the supplier team.<br>It may also be appropriate to provide preparatory training for staff involved in this work. |
| The transfer of technology access and support (transfer) is incomplete and compromises the service's delivery during transition. | Internal IT support arrangements for smaller applications can often be ad hoc or support contracts may not easily be transferred to supplier organisations. In addition the client IT team may not have sought to extend existing support contracts as they are aware that a new supplier is due to take them on.<br><br>The above can easily prevent the outsourcing supplier gaining access or support to essential applications they need to support the client organisation. | All application support arrangements should be documented as part of the pre-transition due diligence process.<br><br>This should then be revisited as part of the transition to agree access and support arrangements for the life of the contract. |
| In-house change management resources and skills are insufficient to sustain the transition programme. | Whilst dedicated internal project and programme staff may be appointed to lead the change for the organisation, this role often comes on top of the 'day job' for the majority for HR staff involved. This can compromise the quality of business-as-usual service delivery, the programme's success and place considerable stress on staff. | Whenever possible, staff should be seconded from their day-to-day role. They may also require development to work in the context of a large complex change project. This will allow them to apply their specialist functional understanding as quickly and effectively as possible.<br><br>Where dedicated resource is not available, a realistic prioritisation of work needs to be made available to staff involved in the project. |

Continued overleaf

Continued

| Risk | Detail | Mitigation |
|------|--------|------------|
| Continuity of third-party service provision during the transition is compromised as relationships with suppliers are lost with the transfer. | The Service Provider may propose the introduction of their own third-party suppliers or may be unfamiliar with dealing with the current incumbents. Either situation can lead to disruption of the service they provide. Relationships and well established points of contact get lost as transition progresses. | A clear inventory of supplier relationships that may be impacted should be documented.<br><br>A plan for communicating with each supplier and an approach to handling their contract should be agreed with the outsourcing services supplier.<br><br>This should be implemented in conjunction with the appropriate third-party suppler and procurement professionals from both parties engaged in the outsourcing contract. |
| Loss of key staff during transition, compromising service delivery capability and quality. | Organisations rarely run their activities based on documented processes alone. The information about 'how to get things done' outside of the defined process is vital to the smooth running of the process, and the quality of the service.<br><br>This organisational knowledge will need to be transferred to the supplier if service performance is not to deteriorate during transition. | Key staff at all levels need to be identified at an early stage in the transition process. The search should look beyond senior staff and include a focus on those that have a rich or specialist knowledge about the current HR service and processes.<br><br>The knowledge capture or transfer process is a key transition work stream to ensure that this is retained and codified.<br><br>Once identified, a plan for managing each individual must be developed and discussed with each staff member. It should assess how long their knowledge will be needed for, the impact of them leaving and whether they will transfer, leave or be retained.<br><br>The retention approach may include career progression, bonus payments for defined tasks completed successfully within the transition programme, or retention payments attached defined time periods. |

This section has provided an overview of the key steps and issues that are faced by any HRO provider and client as they shape and implement their deal. Orion Partners have pooled their collective experience in shaping and managing HRO deals into the following best practice guidelines.

***Before an organisation embarks on outsourcing its HR function it should have:***

1. Identified how outsourcing fits with the organisation's overall strategic objectives.

2. Agreed which core strategic competencies must be kept in-house and what can safely be outsourced? This should be supported by a detailed scope definition of what services and activities are to be offered for outsourcing? (see section 4 – Indicative Scope of Services).

3. Identified a complete view of internal HR service delivery costs; the main cost drivers and the potential savings and investment (business case) that will underpin the outsourcing programme.

4. Attempted or assessed 'internal outsourcing' (or in-sourcing) and explored how setting up an in-house shared service function might deliver many of the benefits of outsourcing but with a greater degree of retained control.

5. Identified the technological challenges and solutions that need to be included in the business case as well as determining the extent to which access will be given to the outsourcers IT resources and capability. If so, ensure that the full costs of running and retiring legacy systems been calculated accurately.

6. Developed a clear view about the capabilities and reputation of each of the main outsourcing providers. Who will suit the organisation best in terms of geographic and cultural fit, as well as breadth and depth of service offerings?

7. Standardized and simplified processes and procedures prior to considering outsourcing. If not, then the client risks outsourcing inefficiency and is likely to pay more than is necessary for services.

8. Discussed in detail the concept of outsourcing with customers (employees and business managers) and other key stakeholders in the organisation – will they support an outsourcing initiative?

9. Defined the key success measures that will be used to judge the performance of the outsource provider. What are the main criteria that will be used to select the outsourcing partner? Is a joint venture or special purpose vehicle an appropriate way of structuring the deal?

10. What is the history of the organisation in terms of managing complex transition processes – is there the organisational will to see an outsourcing initiative through to completion?

11. Realistically determined the amount of time, energy and resources needed to successfully implement the service transfer and change organisational culture.

12. Secured the full support and active commitment of the sponsor and top team driving the change not just at the outset but for the duration of the programme.

---

# APPENDIX A: HR BPO DEALS EUROPE >$50M TCV '99–'06

| Primary Vendor | Client Name | Industry Vertical | Signing Date | End Date | Contract Length (months) |
|---|---|---|---|---|---|
| Capita Group | Norfolk County Council | Local government | 27/07/1999 | 27/07/2009 | 120 |
| Hewitt Associates | British Petroleum | Energy and utilities | 01/12/1999 | 31/12/2006 | 84 |
| Accenture Ltd | BT Group plc | Telecommunications | 22/06/2001 | 22/06/2006 | 60 |
| Accenture Ltd | Cable & Wireless | Telecommunications | 17/12/2001 | 17/12/2006 | 60 |
| Capita Group | UK Government Cabinet Office | Central/federal Government | 17/04/2002 | 17/04/2012 | 120 |
| Affiliated Computer Services Inc | Motorola Inc | Telecommunications | 19/12/2002 | 19/12/2012 | 144 |
| Accenture Ltd | Telecom Italia | Telecommunications | 20/12/2002 | 20/12/2009 | 84 |
| IBM Global Services | Proctor & Gamble | Manufacturing | 09/09/2003 | 01/01/2014 | 120 |
| Affiliated Computer Services Inc | General Motors Corp | Manufacturing | 01/10/2003 | 04/11/2010 | 84 |
| ARINSO | Affiliated Computer Services Inc | Technology | 01/10/2003 | 04/11/2008 | 60 |
| Hewitt Associates | Sun Microsystems | Technology | 05/10/2004 | 05/10/2009 | 60 |
| Accenture Ltd | Sandvik | Other | 16/11/2004 | 16/11/2014 | 120 |
| Accenture Ltd | BT Group plc | Telecommunications | 02/02/2005 | 01/08/2005 | 120 |
| Hewitt Associates | Marriot International Inc | Services | 14/02/2005 | 14/02/2012 | 84 |

| Primary Vendor | Client Name Corporation | Industry Vertical | Signing Date | End Date | Contract Length |
|---|---|---|---|---|---|
| IBM Global Services | Dana Corporation | Manufacturing | 04/04/2005 | 04/04/2015 | 120 |
| LogicaCMG | Metropolitan Police Authority | Central/Federal Government | 11/04/2005 | 11/04/2012 | 84 |
| Hewitt Associates | Pepsi | Manufacturing | 12/04/2005 | 12/04/2015 | 120 |
| Convergys Corp | Unnamed technology company | Technology | 05/05/2005 | 05/05/2015 | 120 |
| Accenture Ltd | BT Group plc | Telecommunications | 07/07/2005 | 01/08/2010 | 60 |
| Convergys Corp | Whirlpool Corp | Manufacturing | 28/07/2005 | 28/07/2015 | 120 |
| Accenture Ltd | Bank of Ireland | Finance | 12/2005 | 12/2012 | 84 |
| Accenture Ltd | Carillion | Construction | 10/2005 | Undisclosed | Undisclosed |
| Accenture Ltd | Unilever | Manufacturing | 06/2006 | 06/2013 | 84 |
| ARINSO | Bank of America | Finance | 08/2006 | 08/2012 | 72 |
| ARINSO | Repsol YPF | Energy and utilities | 05/2006 | 05/2011 | 60 |
| ADP | Ikea | Retail | 07/2006 | Undisclosed | Undisclosed |
| Agilsys | Rochdale Metropolitan Borough Council | Local Government | 04/2006 | 04/2021 | 180 |
| Capita Group | BBC | Media/broadcasting | 02/2006 | 02/2016 | 120 |
| Fujitsu | Northern Ireland Dept. of Finance & Personnel | Central/federal Government | 04/2006 | 04/2021 | 180 |
| Hewitt | Centrica | Energy and utilities | 7/2006 | 12/2013 | 90 |
| Xansa | Lloyds TSB | Finance | 08/2006 | 08/2011 | 60 |

*Source: Orion Partners research*

# APPENDIX B: CASE STUDIES

## *CASE STUDY 1. BRITISH TELECOM/ACCENTURE*

The HRO deal signed in 2000 was one of the first comprehensive outsourcing agreements in Europe. It also utilized a joint venture structure, with BT and Accenture partnering to form e-peopleserve.

### *Drivers for change*
For BT the 2000 deal was the culmination of a 10-year long process. In 1990, its 250 000 employees were served by 14,500 HR professionals, using 26 separate HR systems, 30 telephone help lines and more than 26 physical HR sites aligned to the organisation's geographic districts.

Aside from cost, the pace of change in the telecommunications industry was the key driver for a new approach. Throughout the 1990s, when the business as a whole was undergoing huge restructuring which saw the workforce reduced to about 96 000 in the UK, BT restructured its HR function, organising around business functions rather than geographies, consolidating HR systems and reducing the number of physical sites. In 1998, BT moved to a shared services model for transactional HR in a bid to improve customer service, reduce cost and increase productivity.

### *Deal structure*
The success of the shared service strategy led BT to believe that it could commercialise the HR transformation knowledge it had accumulated throughout its own journey. Ultimately, Accenture approached BT with the idea of building an HRO organisation that would build on BT's experience in HR transaction services and Accenture's expertise in business transformation and technology.

The resulting joint venture, e-peopleserve, set about building an end-to-end HR solution for the employee lifecycle, from hiring and training through performance, reward, employee relations, health and safety to exit. Approximately 1100 BT staff transferred to e-peopleserve, leaving 600 HR executives within BT to concentrate on strategic people issues.

### *Outcomes and lessons*
Getting buy-in within BT was critical for such a significant investment. The HR team highlighted the opportunity to release resources from transactional work to higher value strategic projects, as well as cost savings, better service to employees and wider career choice.

Initially costs went up; in 2002 when the partnership was dissolved, BT found itself paying £80 million against a projected cost of service of £75 million. While reasons for the costs overruns are not clear, BT has admitted that one of the biggest blocks in the early days was the attitude of the HR personnel who were most affected; the general workforce had already been introduced to the shared services concept and were less concerned.

The transferred workforce also took time to adjust to their role as a Service Provider to BT and other companies. Initially they lacked the experience and skills to deliver service and cost improvements. Over time this has been addressed through staff development and process improvement activities led by internal teams of process consultants.

Accenture bought out BT's share of e-peopleserve for US$70 million in 2002 (with an earn-out opportunity valued at between US$35 million and US$222 million over the next 5 years) and rebranded it Accenture HR Services.

Whatever the teething problems, BT are clear about the benefits that outsourcing has delivered:

- One telephone number now exists for staff to contact HR;
- A single Peoplesoft HRIS system provides enhanced HR reporting capability and employee self service;
- A company-wide Docent Learning Management System has been implemented globally;
- BT has been able to move to 1:200 HR staff to employees, well ahead of the benchmarks in its sector;
- Key HR processes have achieved ISO 9001 accreditation;
- Centralised resourcing contracts are delivering savings of £1.2m per annum;
- Jobs can now be offered within 24 hours, rather than up to 12 weeks.

Further savings and process improvements have been released by the offshoring of elements of the recruitment process to Accenture's facilities in Mumbai, India. This occurred in 2003–2004 and was one of the first offshore BPO projects completed.

In February 2005, the initial 5-year term was renewed for a further 10 years, expanding the scope to 37 other countries around the globe in a deal worth US$575 million. It is notable however, that the technology component of the deal was returned to BT, with the PeopleSoft implementation and maintenance now a retained function.

# CASE STUDY 2. BP/HEWITT (FORMERLY EXULT)

## Drivers for change

BP was ahead of its time when it decided to outsource all non-strategic HR functions in the late 1990s. Oil prices were low and BP needed to cut costs. At the same time, it was going through a major buying spree, acquiring multiple HR processes that required rationalisation, as well as the critical mass of employees to make outsourcing viable.

## Deal structure

BP already had experience in outsourcing its IT and finance functions, but at that time HR outsourcing on the scale planned was a world first; the only outsourcing firm who pitched for the work was PricewaterhouseCoopers. In the end, BP gave the contract to a start-up called Exult, taking a 9% interest.

The initial contract required Exult to take over general HR administration, payroll, benefits, retiree administration, relocation service and HR information services and also to manage any other HR outsourcers globally. Exult had 14 months from signing to deliver 20% cost savings.

## Outcomes and lessons

The timescales proved far too ambitious for the scale of the task. BP's various entities and acquisitions were running a multitude of policies and procedures – in the UK alone BP had over 100 different employment contracts. The outsourcing deal required BP and Exult to agree the best of each process then simultaneously move all employees onto the chosen model, to be run out of one of two new shared service centres (one in Houston for US staff, the other in Glasgow for UK). However, in the time available many duplicate processes simply had to be 'lifted and shifted'. Streamlining is still ongoing – in 2003 there were 10 employment contracts in use.

In other areas the original vision proved unworkable; originally the intent was for Exult to cover employees worldwide. However, while it was cost-effective to deliver payroll and other administrative tasks for multiple English-speaking countries, service centres to serve non-English speaking populations required a critical mass of 5000 employees. Eventually the goal of worldwide coverage was dropped.

Other problems stemmed from the language of the contract; Exult and BP agreed to split any savings from managing other outsourcers 50/50 but the cost-savings formula was too imprecise to be workable, so BP employees had no incentive to use approved outsourcers. New formulae were eventually worked out on a case-by-case basis, before a generic solution was developed.

The problems faced by BP and Exult are largely a reflection of the very steep learning curve that both sides had to go up in what was then uncharted territory. The lessons, in terms of understanding the scope before performance measures are agreed, are clear.

Many of the original goals have been achieved, including streamlining of processes and better management information for BP executives on every level from total HR spend to the ability to match employee expertise and goals with company initiatives. According to Hewitt, which acquired Exult in 2004, BP has now achieved significantly in excess of the 20% saving on its baseline annual costs but there is still speculation that BP may nevertheless switch providers. The original contract was due to expire in December 2006 but Hewitts and BP recently announced an 18 month extension to the contract through to 2008. It is widely understood that this symbolises BP's intent to either switch contract to another provider or to take many aspects of the service back in-house (as they did in 2004 to the pensions administration which was previously run by AON). BP is reluctant to switch its HRO provider during 2006/07 because of the complexity of change happening within HR as a global HR SAP system is implemented.

## CASE STUDY 3. ARMED FORCES PERSONNEL AND ADMINISTRATION AGENCY/EXCELLERATEHRO

### Drivers for change
The AFPAA was originally established in 1998 with the objective of consolidating HR services among the three services, as a direct result of cuts in defence spending in 1995 and the general government initiative to seek alternative ways of funding infrastructure improvements.

### Deal structure
The AFPAA's original brief was to gather metrics and undertake benchmarking to understand the military's HR, followed by harmonisation and standardisation as a preliminary to outsourcing which was slated for 2001. In the event, the AFPAA skipped straight to signing a 10 year £600 million outsourcing contract with EDS (now ExcellerateHRO).

The complex contract, which includes 23 schedules and specifies 1800 outputs, required ExcellerateHRO, amongst other things, to take responsibility for a 300 000 staff payroll, administer 500 000 personnel records and 800 000 pension records. 75% of AFPAA's staff were transferred to ExcellerateHRO, which began taking over HR functions only 2 months after signing the deal.

### Outcomes and lessons
Almost inevitably, the rush to outsource created difficulties. Insufficient work had been done to win the buy-in of the three services, and the resistance to changing some very venerable traditions had been overlooked. At the same time, failure to carry out appropriate benchmarking and inventory of existing systems meant that cost-savings did not materialise as quickly as expected and the high expectations of customers were not met.

It took more than 3 years and the commitment of the leaders of all three services, who were by then under additional pressure to cut costs, to achieve real cost savings. It is only now, 8 years after the formation of AFPAA, that the focus can shift on a transformational programme to provide a standardised HRMS package with self-service capability and reduce HR headcount from 1800 to 1000.

Aside from the requirement to establish the baseline and get appropriate buy-in from stakeholders, the head of the AFPAA counsels against relying on HRO providers to deliver solutions to internal problems. While providers can offer advice and experience, a partnership approach is required, particularly where there is a unique organisational culture in play.

## CASE STUDY 4. WESTMINSTER CITY COUNCIL/VERTEX

### Drivers for change
Westminster City Council began to consider outsourcing when a survey revealed that only 50% of their customers (including businesses, residents, staff and visitors) were satisfied with the service they received, despite the Council receiving an excellent rating from the Audit Commission. The core problem was that there were at least five main access routes (phone, email and so on) to seven basic council services. The multiple points of contact and lack of clarity about where to direct specific enquiries was leading to customer dissatisfaction and causing uncertainty about how and when services were being delivered.

The Council wanted a business process transformation and conceived the Customer Service Initiative (CSI) to improve the quality of customers' experience when they contacted the Council. The vision was to reduce numerous customer contacts to deal with a problem to one. A secondary objective is to reduce the cost per customer contact.

### Deal structure
Westminster accepted a consortium bid led by Vertex after a tendering process. Vertex had the experience of large scale CRM from its utilities background together with experience in change management and business process re-engineering that the Council lacked. As prime contractor, Vertex is responsible for programme management, contact centre services, administration and HR services and business process transformation. Vertex has sub-contract agreements with Accord for facilities management, procurement and transportation and with Cap Gemini Ernst & Young for IT facilities management services and CRM design and build and ongoing support.

The contract signed in mid-2002 has an initial value of approximately £282 million over 10 years with opportunities for Vertex to win up to £200 million more when further phases are let. The target savings over the lifetime of the initial 10-year period are £35 million.

A partnership approach has been adopted between the Council and Vertex, with members of both organisations sitting on a partnership management board and the CSI Joint board. The Council identifies this governance structure, together with a jointly agreed vision and code of behaviour and co-location of management teams as critical to the success of the project.

---

### Outcomes and lessons

Westminster has adopted what it calls the 'T-shaped' council. The top of the T is the client interface, allowing customers a choice of access routes to a single point of contact in a customer service centre. The down stroke of the T allows generic transactional processes to sit alongside frontline contact, increasing the ability to resolve issues at first contact and to manage peaks and troughs in demand.

The contract has been successful in increasing customer satisfaction, although at one point ran into an employee relations crisis with threatened strike action over a proposed relocation of work to the north of Scotland. Under the original agreement Council staff were transferred under TUPE to Vertex but given a promise that they would continue working in Westminster until 2012. Of the staff that transferred to Vertex, less than 50 were associated with the HR part of the deal. The Council has now apparently asked Vertex to vacate the space in which staff is housed, with Vertex claiming that its only option within the contract price is to move operations to an existing call centre in Scotland.

Aside from this relatively minor glitch, both sides judge the venture a success, and Vertex aims to market the solution to other councils, with Westminster taking a share in profits from future sales.

## CASE STUDY 5. UNILEVER/ACCENTURE

### Drivers for Change

Unilever is a truly global giant with operations in over 100 countries, revenues of US$60 billion and an employee headcount of 208 000. The company accounts for an array of household brand names and as a result has had to learn how to meet the operational challenges faced by its sheer size and complexity.

In 2005, Unilever's top management began to realise that staying competitive would require a significant reduction in its back office administration routines. A company wide initiative was established with a US$900 million cost cutting target the achievement of which could only be met by a major commitment to business process outsourcing.

### Deal Structure

The BPO process began with Unilever announcing a deal in December 2005 with IBM covering finance and accounting followed by a deal with Accenture in April 2006 to handle their European IT Services. Finally, in June 2006, Unilever announced their US$1 billion HRO contract with Accenture covering the entire enterprise.

The scope of the contract covers all of Unilever's HR transactions and includes recruitment, payroll administration, reward administration, performance management, workforce reporting, core HR administration and third party management services. Accenture will deploy and manage HR software applications and provide content sourcing and development, programme planning and delivery, learning system hosting and management of administrative services as part of the training provision. Globally, Unilever expect about 50% of their 3300 HR staff to be affected by the change.

### Outcomes and Lessons
Unilever are now at the point of moving from decision making to execution so it is still too early to draw meaningful conclusions other than around the vendor selection and management process itself.

During vendor selection, Unilever's HR team worked hard to ensure that the successful vendor could 'walk the talk' as well as demonstrating the ability to work well with the Unilever culture. A great deal of time was spent with reference clients including detailed structured interviews and numerous site visits. Discussion also took place with their own competitors in order to share similar experiences and difficulties.

Going forward, vendor management is the next challenge for Unilever. A common problem in each of the previous deals early phases was that their own staff were unable to keep pace with those of their providers activities resulting in governance dominated by the vendor.

A further challenge is the planned significant shift in people responsibility back to line management for a range of transactions which are key to the delivery of the major productivity gains needed to make the transition successful.

## CASE STUDY 6. LLOYDS TSB XANSA

### Drivers for Change
Lloyds TSB's HR function managed a successful shared service operation for almost 10 years, along the way outsourcing payroll administration to Ceridian, Flexible benefit administration to Towers Perrin (although a current project is underway to in source this back into the company's Registrars business) and replacing its HR delivery platform with Oracle's ERP product.

However, increasing competition in the marketplace and business strategy focused on consolidation within the UK inevitably meant greater pressure to further reduce the Bank's cost: income ratio – a key sector efficiency indicator.

Alongside a strategic HR objective to improve the HR:employee ratio to best in class levels led to the conclusion that significant outsourcing was the only means of meeting the challenge.

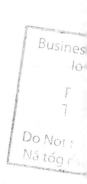

### Deal Structure

Xansa were awarded the contract from a shortlist rumoured to include both Accenture and IBM. Xansa already has number of contracts with Lloyds TSB including finance and accounting transaction processing. The 5-year deal marks Xansa's entry into the HR outsourcing market and whist TCV has not been revealed it is thought to be significant.

Xansa will provide HR services including administration and recruitment and will take over existing helpdesks for training, advice and guidance as well as general enquiries. Xansa will also provide application support (both maintenance and development) for HR's main platform including payroll, although payroll administration remains with Ceridian.

Xansa will deliver the service from Mumbai where around 150 new jobs will be created.

### Outcomes and Lessons

As with Unilever, Lloyds TSB has only recently moved into delivery but there are high expectations that the change will deliver benefit rapidly.

A major challenge for Xansa has certainly been knowledge transfer in areas where bespoke and heavily customized systems are used. Early engagement by Xansa's technical teams was necessary in order to fully understand requirements as well gain as much understanding as possible before key HR staff moved on. Clearly, understanding of the Oracle infrastructure appears not to have presented difficulty but no doubt Xansa will be treading wearily as they drill deeper into complexity.

Lloyds TSB still have to resolve the best technical solution for their ageing payroll system and will no doubt be looking to Xansa to help them determine the most appropriate way forward in the context of this deal.

Overall, the project thus far has been considered a success, well received by the business and staff through a major change management push .The challenge now facing HR and Xansa is successful service transition in the face of challenging service KPI's already in place with the business.


# CASE STUDY 7. BBC/CAPITA


### Drivers for Change

The BBC is under increasing pressure to increase efficiency through a series of 'value for money' initiatives designed to drive out further cost savings in order to release funds into programming.

Centralisation of transactional services across the corporations 17 different business divisions has already taken place with £20 million having been taken out of HR's cost base of £80 million over the last 3 years with a significant reduction in HR headcount. During this period, staff attitude to change appeared to harden with a recent poll suggesting that the majority felt that the BBC had become disjointed following outsourcing deals, hindering the drive towards greater collaboration.

Against this background, the BBC's HR function were not only looking for an outsourcing vendor who could deliver further process re-engineering benefit but also handle the significant shift in employee mindset towards change as well as support the corporations strategic goal of becoming the world's most creative media organisation.

### The Deal

Capita beat Xchanging to the £100 million 10-year deal which covers recruitment administration, pay administration (excluding pensions), some elements of staff development, occupational health and various HR related administrative areas.

Over the next 3 years, HR staffing is planned to fall back to 450 with around 260 jobs being outsourced, 180 redundancies and others being redeployed elsewhere across the Corporation. It is anticipated that savings of around £50 million will be generated over the 10-year deal.

The deal, whist considered very large, is not a total (full service) HRO with some industry commentators feeling that it may well be sometime before the UK witnesses a full HR outsourcing deal given the reluctance of organisations to relinquish all responsibility for people matters.

### Outcome and Lessons

Capita certainly have the capability to drive out more value for the BBC but it remains to be seen whether there is sufficient appetite to see further significant cuts to HR services already perceived to have been hit hard. Arguably, their greatest challenge is shifting culture to where there is a greater understanding of the importance of the customer, establishing their needs and delivering to them.

The BBC has already run into industrial relations over their plan to shift around 100 jobs to Capita's service centre in Belfast. Assurances have been given that staff who do not wish to move to Belfast will be re-deployed to a Capita office near their current location, although the trade unions have objected to staff being asked to work on non-BBC Capita work.

# APPENDIX C: LEADING PROVIDER PROFILES

## *PROVIDER PROFILE – ACCENTURE*

### Key Data
- Headquartered in New York, NY
- Headcount: c100 000
- Founded in 1947 by Arthur Andersen
- 2005 Sales: US$15.5 billion
- 2005 Net Income: US$940 million

### Clients
- Australia's Victorian State Government
- Bank of Ireland
- Best Buy Corp.
- Bristol-Myers Squibb
- British Telecom (BT)
- Borden Chemical
- Carillion
- Cable & Wireless
- City of Copenhagen
- New Century Financial Corp.
- Sandvik
- Telecom Italia
- Unilever
- US Transportation Security Administration
- Victoria State Government

### Scope of Service
- Accenture HR Services uses a third party platform to provide payroll services using a third party for the benefits platform. Accenture's preferred approach is to build a new platform and deploy new processes rather than use the client's existing platform.
- Approximate global market share of US$4.9 billion in TCV.
- Market share of ci12% in terms of employees supported.
- Global geographical presence covers North America, Central/Latin America, South America, EMEA and Asia Pacific.
- Scope of services: Customer contact services, exit services, management information, learning, managed HR services, performance management, recruitment, pay and reward.
- Target client size: small (5000)–large (75 000+).

### Strengths
- Financial strength as part of Accenture.
- More than 15 years of BPO experience in finance, procurement and IT.
- Significant credibility on the IT side of HR and strong ERP capability.
- Significant pool of subject matter expertise.
- Global presence.
- Strong relationships with technology partners.
- HRO business has access to Accenture clients.

### Challenges

- Faces strong competition from traditional HR vendors with deep domain specialisation.
- Poor penetration in government market particularly in the UK.

### Recent Deals

- The Unilever deal is the largest contract awarded at US$1billion on an annual billing basis. The deal includes recruitment, payroll administration, reward administration, performance management, workforce reporting, core HR administration and third party management services.
- In this deal with the Bank of Ireland both HRO and procurement are in-scope, the basis of which is a wholesale transformation of the HR function including learning.
- The contract with Sandvik expands an existing 10-year contract signed in 2004 with Accenture providing application and development services for their existing Peoplesoft platform including helpdesk support.

# PROVIDER PROFILE – AFFILIATED COMPUTER SERVICES

### Key Data

- Headquartered in Dallas, Texas
- Headcount: c43 000 (75% U.S.)
- Founded in 1988 as a financial computer services provider, focused on processing bank transactions
- 2005 Sales: US$4.35 billion
- 2005 Net Income: US$415 million

### Clients

- AT & T
- Blue Cross and Blue Shield
- Chubb & Son
- Delta Air Lines
- Gateway
- General Motors Europe
- Goodyear Tire & Rubber Company
- Motorola
- Rohm and Hass

### Scope of Service

- System and workflow capability.
- Approximate global market share of US$2.5 billion TCV.
- Approximate market share of c13% in terms of employees supported.
- Global geographical presence covers 65 countries throughout North America, Central/Latin America, South America, EMEA, and Asia Pacific.
- Range of services includes recruitment, performance management, pay and reward, learning, succession planning, HR data administration, pension administration, time and attendance, employee relations, exit management, expat /repat and relocation administration, management information.
- Target client size: mid (10 000) – large (10 000 – 75 000+).

---

### Strengths
- Very strong reputation in US public sector.
- Key IT services competencies particularly around PeopleSoft and SAP.
- Global presence and experience delivering large-scale BPO contracts.
- Ability to leverage HR subject matter expertise from resulting from Mellon acquisition.

### Challenges
- Its move into the commercial sector will continue to be a challenge following the sale of a major portion of its U.S. federal government business to Lockheed Martin since more than half its revenue comes from the public sector.
- Successfully complete the integration of Mellon.

### Recent Deals
- Motorola: In February, 2003, ACS and Motorola signed a 10 year US$650 million HR outsourcing contract. Under this agreement, ACS provides services including benefits administration, learning services, relocation, selection and assessment, and other key employee development functions.
- General Motors – Europe: In 2003, ACS and General Motors – Europe (GM-Europe) signed a 7 year US$210 million HR outsourcing contract. Under this agreement, ACS provides recruitment, personnel administration, timekeeping and payroll, expatriate payroll, travel and expense, training, reporting and data archiving to GM's 110 000 European employees.
- Goodyear: Specific services provided include employee and manager self-service, HRIS systems support and maintenance, compensation, payroll, benefits administration, participant call centre, training/e-learning, recruiting and staffing services and systems for the 84 000 Goodyear associates.
- Delta Air Lines committed to a 7 year, US$120 million outsourcing agreement in 2005 with ACS, which will provide compensation and benefits administration, relocation services, recruiting, learning, payroll, HR information services, and employee call centre services.

## PROVIDER PROFILE – FIDELITY EMPLOYER SERVICES COMPANY

### Key Data
- Headquartered in Boston, MA
- Headcount: c9 000

### Clients
- ABB
- Bank of America
- BASF
- Bertelsmann AG
- IBM

---

## Scope of Service

- Approximate global market share of US$1.5 billion TCV.
- Approximate market share of c 12% employees supported.
- Global geographical presence covers North America and EMEA.
- Scope of services: defined contribution, defined benefits, health & welfare, HR/payroll.
- Target client size: mid (10 000) – large (75 000+).

## Strengths

- Long established competitor in HR BPO serving more than 250 000 employees.
- Strong presence in the US and Europe position the company well to leverage value from its financial services capability.
- Financially, Fidelity's proprietary model is attractive because it is a single, standardized platform with scale economies making it 'price competitive'.
- Has a 'multi-client system strategy' with all clients benefiting from enhancements that satisfy broad base of user requirements.

## Challenges

- Most customers are still using Oracle applications for their other HR services presenting it with a major task in migrating users onto its HR Access platform.
- Fidelity has a proprietary platform making it hard to be as flexible as some companies may wish.

## Recent Deals

- ABB selected Fidelity in 2004 to deliver personnel records administration, compensation planning, payroll, H&W and benefits administration, HR reporting for 115 000 employees.
- Bank of America contracted Fidelity in 2004 for 7 years to perform compensation, performance management, talent management, learning, payroll, time and attendance, personnel administration, employee record maintenance, HRIS, H&W and benefit administration for 250 000 active and retired employees.
- BASF signed a 5-year deal in 2005 with Fidelity to serve 20 000 active and retired employees with the following services: payroll, H&W and retirement plans.
- IBM selected Fidelity in 2002 for 10 years to perform health plan administration, career services and pension administration for 260 000 employees.

## PROVIDER PROFILE – HEWITT (EXULT)

### Key Data
- Headquartered in Lincolnshire, IL
- Headcount: c17 000
- Founded by Ted Hewitt in 1940
- 2005 Sales: US$2.84 billion
- 2005 Net Income: US$135 million

### Clients
- Air Canada
- Baylor Health
- Cap Gemini Ernst & Young
- Centrica
- Circuit City
- Duke Energy Corp.
- EDS
- Group Semco
- Marriott International Inc.
- Mervyn's
- Omnicom
- PepsiCo
- Prudential Financial Corporation
- Sun Microsystems
- Rockwell Automation
- Thomson
- TXU
- Unisys
- Wachovia
- Warner Music Group

### Scope of Service
- Hewitt Associates has expanded its services offerings through the acquisitions of Cyborg Systems (payroll services), Northern Trust Retirement Consulting (retirement and health administrative services) and pension administration from Royal Philips Electronics.
- Exult has its own self-service capabilities built around HR service delivery with ERP capability.
- Approximate global market share of US$7.8 billion in TCV.
- Market share of c21% in terms of employees supported.
- Global geographical presence covers North America, Central/Latin America, EMEA and Asia Pacific.
- Scope of services: benefits, health & welfare, pension administration, HR BPO, payroll, workforce management.
- Target client size mid (10 000)–large (75 000+).

### Strengths
- Market leader after acquisition of Exult and has significant domain experience.
- Pay and reward competency.

- Offers a compelling value proposition; reputation for quality has an experienced consulting base and leverages value from a proprietary platform.
- Extensive public sector experience and penetration in the US.

### Challenges
- Likely to come under strong competition from the large IT Service organisations when large system integration work is involved.
- As yet to make significant breakthrough in the European market.
- Reluctance in the UK to move into the large public sector market because of perceived complexity and lengthy timescales.

### Recent Deals
- In July 2006 agreed a 7.5-year deal with the energy supplier Centrica to undertake workforce administration, reward management, customer service, performance management and succession planning covering 30 000 employees in the UK.
- Rockwell Automation contracted Hewitt in 2005 for 15 years to perform workforce administration, payroll, health and welfare and defined benefit services for 15 000 employees.
- Sun Microsystems signed a 5-year deal in 2004 with Hewitt to serve 30 000 employees with the following services: Workforce administration, recruiting, compensation, performance management and learning.
- Marriott International selected Hewitt in 2005 for 7 years to perform HRIS, compensation, benefits, recruiting, domestic relocation and learning and development for 128 000.
- PepsiCo chose Hewitt Associates for a 10-year deal in April 2005 to focus on HR business process outsourcing services such as workforce and benefits administration, payroll and contact centre support. The deal also includes HR application development and hosting services for 64 000 of the food and beverage giant's U.S. employees and 38 000 international employees.

## PROVIDER PROFILE – IBM

### Key Data
- Headquartered in Armonk, NY
- Headcount: c330 000
- Founded in 1914 by Thomas Watson
- 2005 Sales: US$91 billion
- 2005 Net Income: US$8 billion

### Clients
- Allianz Life Korea
- Banco Santander Totta
- Banco Sabadell
- Cigna
- Dana Corp.
- Lincoln Financial
- NiSource
- Proctor and Gamble
- Williams

## Scope of Service

- Strongest IT Services offering in the marketplace.
- Approximate global market share of US$1.3 billion in TCV.
- Approximate market share of c7% in terms of employees supported.
- Global geographical presence covers North America, Central/Latin America, EMEA and Asia Pacific.
- Scope of services: full HR transaction processing, payroll, web-enabled self-service, contact centres, recruitment, learning, expatriate services.
- Target client size: med (10,000)–large (75 000+).

## Strengths

- IBM has global delivery capability in large-scale transaction-based services, executed by shared service centres spanning all continents.
- Market leading competencies with all ERP software applications as well as middleware skills to integrate multiple applications, tools and databases.

## Challenges

- Potential branding issue in the HR marketplace as many firms continue to associate IBM with IT rather than possessing real HR domain expertise.
- The company's relationship with Fidelity may become strained with issues surrounding deployment and migration of HR Access.
- HR domain knowledge – has been looking for a partner (for example, Mercer).

## Recent Deals

- IBM acquired the business process outsourcing services provider Equitant in order to raise its presence in what is becoming a key growth market.
- IBM and LogicaCMG have together been awarded a contract to develop the Human Resource Management (HRM) Shared Service Centre (P-Direkt) for the Dutch Ministry of the Interior and Kingdom Relations (BZK).
- Cigna signed a 7-year deal in 2004 with IBM to serve 28 000 employees with benefits, payroll, HR services, implementing new HR systems.
- Proctor & Gamble agreed a US$400 million with IBM in 2003 for 10 years to perform application development & management of the HR systems, including payroll processing, benefits administration, compensation planning, expatriate and relocation services, travel and expense management, and HR data management for 98 000 employees.

*Source: Orion Partners research*

# APPENDIX D: SCOPE OF SERVICES

| PROCESS | ACTIVITY | HR BP | COE | SSC | Employee | Manager | 3rd Party | In Scope for Outsourcing? | Country Exceptions |
|---|---|---|---|---|---|---|---|---|---|
| Employee Data/ record management | Employee data record update | | | | | | | Y | |
| | Maintenance of HRIS systems reporting hierarchies | | | | | | | Y | |
| | Records/ file maintenance (inc document scanning | | | | | | | Y | |
| | Compliance and reporting | | | | | | | Y | |
| | | | | | | | | | |
| Travel and expenses | Expense claim processing | | | | | | | Y | |
| | Expense record management | | | | | | | Y | |
| | Reimbursement and cost allocation | | | | | | | Y | |
| | | | | | | | | | |
| Payroll | On cycle pay | | | | | | | Y | |
| | Off cycle pay | | | | | | | Y | |
| | One off payments | | | | | | | Y | |
| | Tax calculation and reporting | | | | | | | Y | |
| | Disbursements | | | | | | | Y | |
| | Accounting to general ledger | | | | | | | Y | |
| | HM Revenue and Customs reporting | | | | | | | Y | |
| | Year end management (P11d, P60) | | | | | | | Y | |
| | | | | | | | | | |
| Benefits | Enrolment and options administration | | | | | | | Y | |
| | Plan administration | | | | | | | Y | |
| | Record maintenance | | | | | | | Y | |
| | Claims administration | | | | | | | Y | |
| | 3rd party management and liaison | | | | | | | Y | |
| | Car fleet management admin | | | | | | | Y | |
| | Pension administration | | | | | | | Y | |
| | | | | | | | | | |
| Compensation | Salary administration | | | | | | | Y | |
| | Bonus administration | | | | | | | Y | |
| | Stock option/ Restricted share administration | | | | | | | Y | |
| | Savings plan administration | | | | | | | Y | |
| | Total rewards statements | | | | | | | Y | |
| | Executive compensation planning and administration | | | | | | | N | |
| | Reward policies and strategy | | | | | | | N | |
| | | | | | | | | | |
| Performance Management | Performance review cycle administration | | | | | | | Y | |
| | Absence monitoring | | | | | | | Y | |
| | Absence management | | | | | | | Y | |
| | Disciplinary and grievance record management | | | | | | | Y | |
| | Interpretation of policy and practice around disciplinary and grievance processes | | | | | | | N | |
| | Industrial tribunal/ legal support | | | | | | | N | |
| | | | | | | | | | |
| Learning and development (including | Development review process cycle administration | | | | | | | Y | |
| | Learning plan maintenance | | | | | | | Y | |
| | Catalogue maintenance | | | | | | | Y | |
| | Demand management (scheduling) | | | | | | | Y | |
| | 3rd party sourcing management | | | | | | | Y | |
| | Delivery of training | | | | | | | Y | |
| | Evaluation and assessment | | | | | | | Y | |
| | Training record administration | | | | | | | Y | |
| | Competency model development and maintenance | | | | | | | N | |
| | Standard training needs analysis | | | | | | | N | |
| | Career pathing and succession planning | | | | | | | N | |
| | Talent management administration | | | | | | | N | |
| | High flier development programme design and delivery | | | | | | | N | |
| | Design of training solutions | | | | | | | N | |
| | Coaching and mentoring | | | | | | | N | |
| | Strategic needs analysis | | | | | | | N | |
| | Identification of high-fliers | | | | | | | N | |
| | Talent management/ Executive succession | | | | | | | N | |
| | | | | | | | | | |
| Relocation | Relocation query handling | | | | | | | Y | |
| | Policy briefing and administration | | | | | | | Y | |
| | Expenses processing and accounting | | | | | | | Y | |
| | Inventory management | | | | | | | Y | |
| | Relocation assistance (physical move support) | | | | | | | Y | |
| | | | | | | | | | |
| Global mobility | Pre-departure administration and advice | | | | | | | N | |
| | On assignment support and administration | | | | | | | N | |
| | Visa and work permit administration | | | | | | | N | |
| | Repatriation management | | | | | | | N | |
| | Post repatriation support | | | | | | | N | |
| | | | | | | | | | |
| Exit | Exit administration | | | | | | | Y | |
| | Voluntary exit administration | | | | | | | Y | |
| | Involuntary exit administration | | | | | | | Y | |
| | Exit data services (payroll and pensions data updates) | | | | | | | Y | |
| | Redundancy and severance programme administration | | | | | | | Y | |
| | Outplacement support | | | | | | | Y | |
| | Exit interviews and analysis | | | | | | | N | |
| | Exit/ severance decisions | | | | | | | N | |
| | | | | | | | | | |
| Management reporting | General HR and management report support | | | | | | | Y | |
| | Team and individual reports | | | | | | | Y | |
| | Report writing services | | | | | | | Y | |
| | Standard monthly reporting | | | | | | | Y | |
| | Trend analysis | | | | | | | Y | |
| | Surveys | | | | | | | Y | |
| | | | | | | | | | |
| Vendor/ 3rd party management | Service management and reporting | | | | | | | N | |
| | Supplier sourcing and procurement | | | | | | | Y | |
| | Invoicing and accounts | | | | | | | Y | |
| | | | | | | | | | |
| Recruiting (internal and external) | Recruitment administration | | | | | | | | |
| | Graduate recruitment activities | | | | | | | N | |
| | Senior management recruitment (specialized search agencies) | | | | | | | Y | |
| | Executive recruitment (specialized search agencies) | | | | | | | Y | |
| | Recruitment/ resource planning | | | | | | | Y | |
| | Authority to recruit | | | | | | | N | |
| | Final interviews | | | | | | | N | |
| | Selection decisions | | | | | | | N | |
| | Offer package sign-off | | | | | | | N | |
| | | | | | | | | | |
| Policy and Strategy | Corporate strategic planning, goal setting and forecasting | | | | | | | N | |
| | HR policy development and design | | | | | | | N | |
| | Legal compliance monitoring | | | | | | | N | |
| | | | | | | | | | |
| HR business partnering | Strategic advice and support to business unit managers | | | | | | | N | |
| | Business unit strategy and policy design | | | | | | | N | |
| | | | | | | | | | |
| Employee Relations | Union/ employee consultation and negotiation | | | | | | | N | |
| | Collective bargaining activities | | | | | | | N | |

# Index

---